DAY TRADING

DAY TRADING

MOMENTUM, LEVEL 2 AND READING THE TAPE

Advanced trading knowledge about Entries and Exits, Volume, Level 2, Trading Halts, Momentum, False Breakouts and more

ROBERTAS CEPONAS

© 2023 Robertas Ceponas - All rights reserved

All rights reserved. No part of this book may be reproduced or transmitted in any form, or by any means, electronic or mechanical, including photocopying, recording, or any information storage and retrieval system, without prior permission of the Author.

Disclaimer

The author, including its publisher and affiliates, is NOT an investment advisory service, a registered investment advisor or a broker-dealer and does not undertake to advise clients on which securities they should buy or sell for themselves. It must be understood that a very high degree of risk is involved in trading securities. The author, the publisher and the affiliates assume no responsibility or liability for trading and investment results. It should not be assumed that the methods, techniques or indicators presented in the book will be profitable nor that they will not result in losses. In addition, the indicators, strategies, rules and all other features of the book are provided for informational and educational purposes only and should not be construed as investment advice. Examples presented are for educational purposes only. Accordingly, readers should not rely solely on the Information in making any trades or investments. Rather, they should use the Information only as a starting point for doing additional independent research in order to allow them to form their own opinions regarding trading and investments. Investors and traders must always consult with their licensed financial advisors and tax advisors to determine the suitability of any investment.

TABLE OF CONTENTS

CHAPTER 1
HOW TO READ AND UNDERSTAND THE BOOK 1

CHAPTER 2
TERMS OR PHRASES THAT YOU NEED TO UNDERSTAND 4

CHAPTER 3
MOMENTUM TRADING AREAS AND TIME FRAMES 10

CHAPTER 4
STOCK SELECTION 15

CHAPTER 5
FINDING AN UPTREND 26

CHAPTER 6
WHO IS MOVING THE PRICE? 34

CHAPTER 7
HOW TO READ LEVEL 2 39

CHAPTER 8
MOMENTUM ENTRIES ON LEVEL 2 47

CHAPTER 9
IMPORTANT INFORMATION 70

CHAPTER 10
TRADING STOCK HALTS 101

CHAPTER 11
DEALING WITH FALSE BREAKOUTS 109

CHAPTER 12.
EXAMPLE AND MY THOUGHT PROCESS 120

CHAPTER 13
EXAMPLES WITH COMMENTARY 133

AFTERWORD 150

CHAPTER I
HOW TO READ AND UNDERSTAND THE BOOK

First of all, I want you to know that this book came from a compilation of my notes so this is not going to be another basic trading book. I do not sell courses, make videos, post my signals or anything like that. I just want to share my knowledge that I've gained during my trading years.

I read hundreds of trading and day trading books, psychology books, self-discipline books. Watched excessive amount of Youtube videos and all that to become a better trader. But there is so little information about Level 2 and tape reading that I decided to share my knowledge with you.

The core of the book is, as I mentioned, about Level 2, Momentum trading and reading the tape. In addition to that, I have added various chapters of information that would usually be skipped in other trading books.

Level 2 is the most predominant source of information in day trading. Neither charts or any indicators can provide such valuable data as Level 2 does. When I started learning day trading, Level 2 was a mystery, a noise where numbers would make no sense and when I tried to learn more about it - there was no literature about it. It was really hard to write about it because Level 2 is in constant movement and displaying it on the paper took a lot of effort.

Momentum trading is where I found my trading edge. There are many trading strategies and many of them are good ones, but they have never been as successful as momentum trading for me. But you need to understand that the way I describe my strategy is not that simple. It's not as basic as putting a trade on once a price crosses a certain level. You need to read the whole book, understand it, and then apply momentum trading in your own way with the knowledge that I have provided here.

Reading the tape is a cliche in the trading literature. It is usually described as a price action which you need to learn, but does not explain how. And then it will be added that the Tape reading was core piece information for the past traders who made millions. In this book I will actually try to explain how to read it and how I use it in my day trading.

The most important thing to know before reading is that this book is not a step by step tutorial. I want you to understand the methods that I am using might not be suitable for you. Maybe certain strategies will work for you and some will not, but this will definitely change the way you day trade.

Since this book is orientated to advanced day traders, I expect that the reader will have a basic knowledge of day trading. Here is a list of the topics that you should have knowledge about:

- General understanding of trading;
- Support and resistance;
- What is Level 2;

- Candles and their patterns;
- Volume;
- Moving Averages;
- VWAP;
- Float of the stock;

There is so much information about these topics so I will not waste your time and money just by repeating what is written in other books.

Here you can see a list of topics that I will be focusing on:
- How to pick the right stocks for day trading;
- How to trade during the momentum;
- How to look at the volume and its impact to trading;
- How to read the tape;
- How to read Time and Sales;
- Where to find support and resistance;
- False breakouts;
- Trading Halts;
- What Level 2 is telling you;
- What Level 2 is trying to tell you;
- What Level 2 is hiding from you;
- Volatility;
- Hotkeys;
- What tools you need for day trading;
- What indicators to use and not to use;
- Little bit of mental preparation, but not too much.

While some topics might be known to you, I will be providing my take on how I use certain tools for my day trading. Let's get started.

CHAPTER 2
TERMS OR PHRASES THAT YOU NEED TO UNDERSTAND

I do suggest that you read this chapter a few times so you would understand my explanations better. We both might understand the same material, but use different wording for it.

Stocks
Whenever I will be talking about equity, ticker or a company, I will be using the same word - stock. I decided to take this approach to make it more simple for the readers. When you see a word stock, it means I am talking about shares that are traded on the Stock Exchange and have a price.

Price, Price action and Price Levels
These three terms will be repeated many times in this book. You need to understand the concept of them and how they interact with each other. It might sound a little overwhelming at the beginning, but once you understand - it becomes simple as it is. Please note that many people understand and interpret these phrases differently. Here I will explain how I perceive price, price action and price levels.

Price

When I talk about price I am referring to the current price of the stock on a certain chart. Not what is today's price when you are reading the book, but the price shown on the chart.

Image A1

In the *A1* image, you can see the RED line that keeps moving when the stock's price changes. You can see that the current price on this chart is $0.24. This is the Price that I am referring to.

Now, if there is no chart and I say the stock is trading at $2.00 and then I say that the price moved to $3.00, you can imagine that this RED line went up to $3.00, and now it shows $3.00 at the end of it.

Price action
This is a little harder to understand, but simply put - it is the movement of the RED line. On a micro level, when you look at the chart and see this RED line jumping up and down means you are looking at the price action.

DAY TRADING

On the higher scale it has a different meaning. Let's say the stock at 10:00 AM is trading at $5.00 and later on, at 11:30 AM is trading at $6.53. In one hour and thirty minutes the price has changed by $1.53. The footprint that the price left while moving are candles and all of these candles would be the price action on the higher scale.

Let's take a look at the following image (*Image A2*).

Image A2

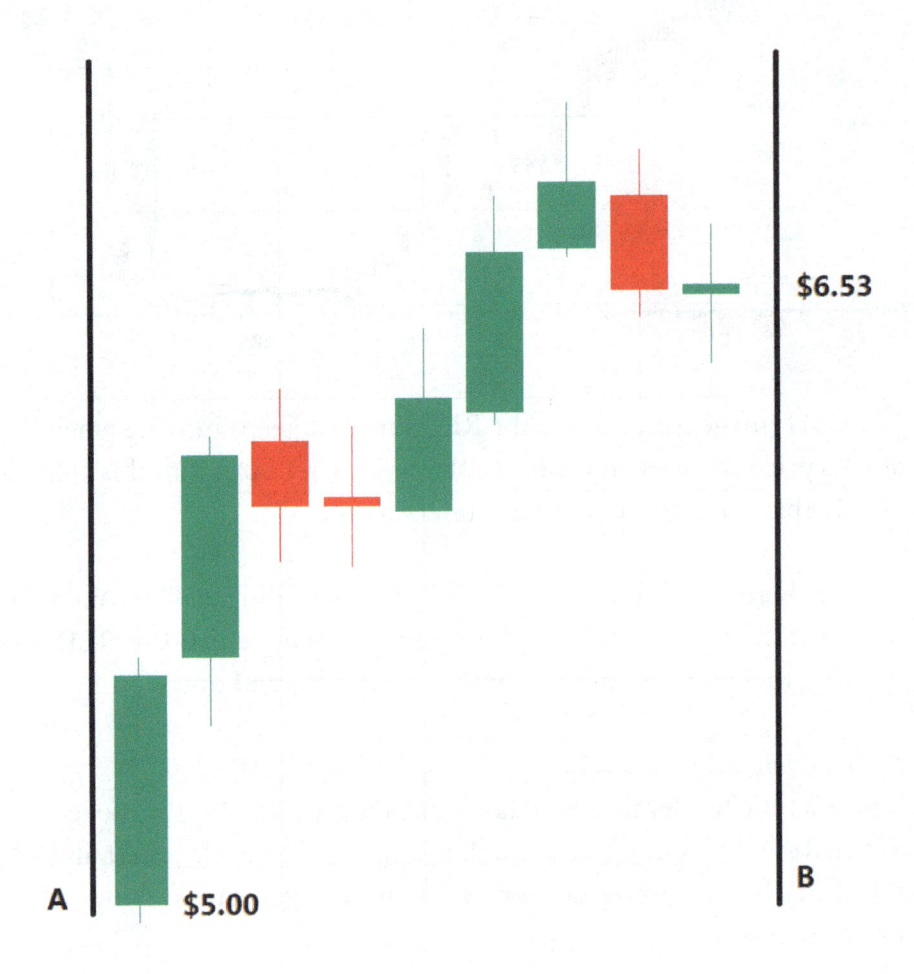

All of the candles that formed between A and B express the price action. It can be any time interval and any time frame. Later on I will explain what clean price action is and not clean price action is.

Most important take from this *A2 image* is that the price action is how the price was moving during a certain period of time. And when we look at the chart and we see the last candle forming - that is part of the price action, because the price action is basically drawing that candle and how all previous candles were drawn.

Price levels and Price areas
Price Levels and Price Areas have a couple of similar meanings. If you look at your chart's Y axis, you will see many prices on it. Here is an example of mine.

Image A3
In this example we have different price levels which start at $13.00 and end at $20.00. Every increment of the price is called a price level. You will read about me saying that we need to wait until price reaches a certain price level. But to be more accurate, any price, literally any price can be called price level. $14.00, $14.59, $14.01, $319.61 all of these prices are price levels. In the most simple way - any price on the Y axis is called a price level or a price area.

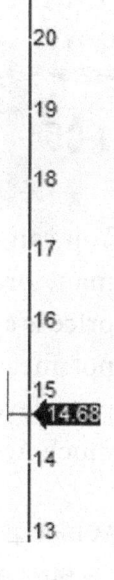

When we will be analysing price levels on Level 2, we will be talking about every single price increment. This is how our Level 2 will look like (*Image A4*).

Image A4

BID	SIZE	ASK	SIZE
1.08	47	1.09	16
1.08	41	1.09	14
1.08	41	1.09	10
1.08	38	1.09	10
1.08	38	1.09	5
1.08	38	1.09	5
1.08	7	1.10	45
1.08	4	1.10	2
1.08	2	1.10	2
1.07	36	1.10	1
1.06	32	1.11	60
1.05	25	1.12	48

You can see on the top left (BID) the price is at $1.08, then there are many orders, then the next price down is $1.07, then $1.06 etc. Each price is a price level. Just because there are many orders at $1.08 it does not mean that there are many price levels at $1.08, it's still just one price level. If you are still struggling to understand, do not worry too much, we will dig deeper into Level 2 later in this book.

When I will be talking about price areas, I will be talking about a certain price with some deviation. Always think about giving some room for the price up and down. Let's look at another example (*Image A5*).

Image A5

The RED line is our Price Action, the YELLOW line is a horizontal line that I placed on the chart manually. When the price (on the chart is $1.04 at the moment) comes to $1.15 price area, I usually mean around $1.13 - $1.17 area. Or when I say that we need to wait until the price is trading in the $8.90 area, you should always think about some room up and down. It's never a set amount.

If you are already familiar with these terms, it won't be hard for you to adapt to my understanding of it.

CHAPTER 3
MOMENTUM TRADING AREAS AND TIME FRAMES

Momentum trading is very well known to many traders where you enter a trade when the price of the stock is surging up and exiting before it starts pulling back. However, not that many traders know when to enter and exit using this strategy.

Let's get few things straight before we deep dive into momentum trading:

- I only trade Long positions and never Short. I suggest you do the same because: you don't need to worry about Short Selling restrictions, Hard to Borrow restrictions and, most importantly, you do not start jumping from long positions to short positions and then back to long positions. You will have plenty of opportunities every single day just by focusing on long positions. (by long I mean you buy the stock and sell it when the price rises, not holding it for long period of time);

- Momentum trading will only work on certain stocks every day. If you don't know how to pick the right stock, this strategy is not going to work. Make sure you read and understand the "Stock selection" chapter. I never have a "list for today" that I am going to trade. I trade stocks that are moving and I join the momentum, and the moment they stop moving, I look for a different stock;

- Low float stocks are my friends. I have read so much misinformation about low float stocks and how "bad" volatility is. Yes, they are volatile and hard to trade, but that's where the money is. While many people are afraid of stocks getting "Halted", I love it. The price went up or down 50% in 5 minutes - I love it. After reading this book and understanding its concept, you will love it too and, hopefully, you will make money out of it.

These are my preferences and I highly suggest you try and apply them to your trading strategy. But do not be afraid and experiment to see what works the best for you. Some traders might find their edge only at shorting or trading large cap stocks. In this book I am explaining what works for me and it is up to you how to use this knowledge.

Momentum trading time frames
Most of you are aware of two most popular chart patterns: ABCD and Bull Flag which are basically the same thing. The price rises, then it pulls back, then it rises again. These two patterns are the foundation of momentum trading.

I use only three types of charts for my momentum trading and look for ABCD/Bull Flag patterns on:
- 1 minute chart;
- 5 minute chart;
- Daily chart. I use Daily charts when looking for stocks to trade, but I don't look for ABCD or Bull Flag on daily charts.

I never look for reasons why the price is rising or why the price is falling because you will never find out. It's either the supply higher than demand or demand higher than the supply. That is all we need to know. If you try to find reasoning, you will never find the right answer because there are too many variables and factors that affect the change of the price.

Image B1

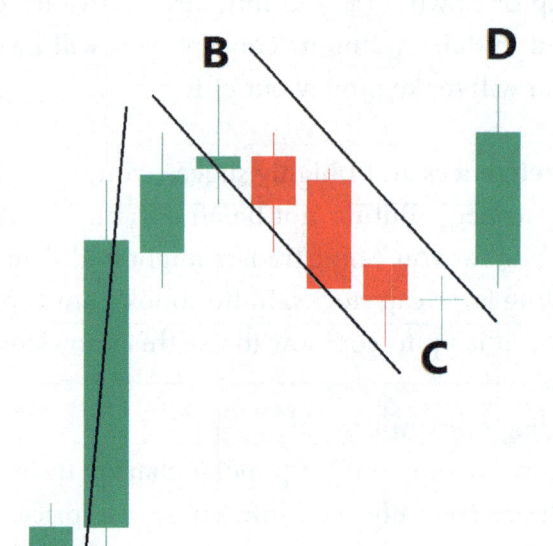

ABCD/Bull Flag pattern

As you can see in the *(Image B1)*, this is a perfect example of the ABCD/Bull Flag pattern. Some people might say it might have too much retracement to be a Bull Flag or there are not enough candles on the pullback to be considered as ABCD, but all what matters to us - **price went up, pulled back and then went up again**. Most of the time this pattern will not be as clean as this.

I know many of you are already thinking that it's easy to draw lines once you have the pattern in front of you and how can you know when to enter and exit trades. I will answer both of these questions in the Level 2 section. For now, let's focus on building the foundation of our strategy.

For momentum trading we trade only when the price is surging up. If we take the same chart as previous and mark where our trade zone is it would look like in this *(Image B2)*.

Image B2

Blue areas are our trading areas

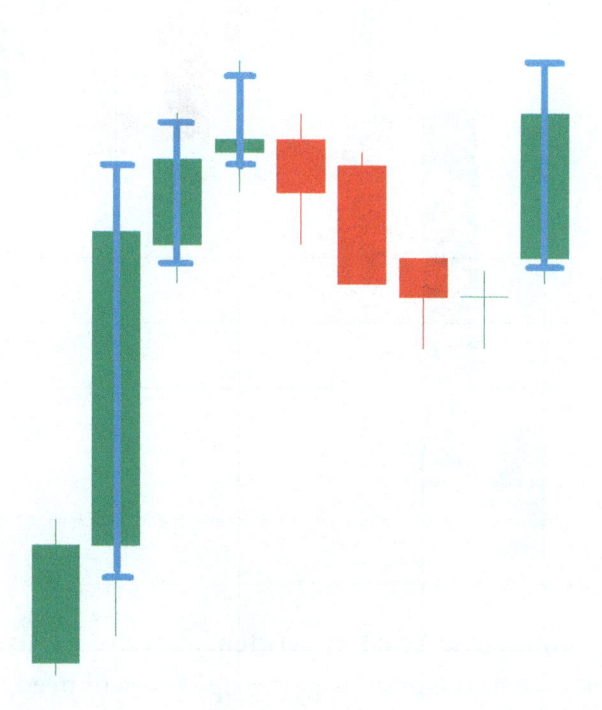

We don't need to catch every move and never expect to do it because we will never know how high or low the price can go. If you put all blue areas together from the *Image B2* in a line and manage to make a trade worth 15-20% percent of that move, you would make a lot of money. And the best part is that your trade can be anywhere within those blue lines. Take a look at this example (*Image B3*), any of these trades in <u>yellow</u> would be good trades.

Image B3

All trades in Yellow are good trades

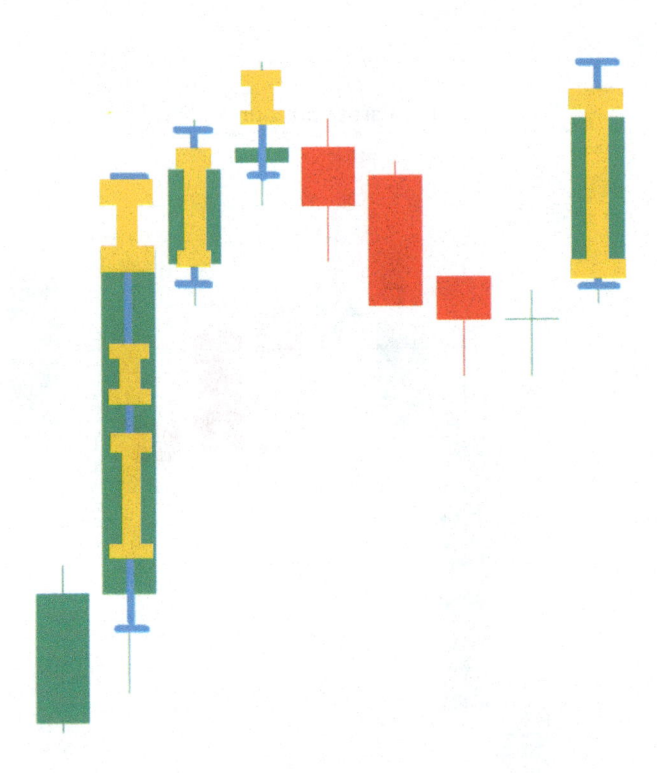

To simply summarise what is written above - we use momentum strategy only when the price is going up. You will need to experiment and figure out which of those areas are the most successful to you, but do not worry, I will provide examples for every type of entry.

CHAPTER 4
STOCK SELECTION

Selecting stocks plays a major role in momentum trading. Without the right stocks you will never be able to be profitable using momentum. I don't know how else I can emphasise how important it is. Do not check other people's lists or Hot Stocks, CNBC or Reddit. I will teach you how to recognize momentum stocks. It takes some time at the beginning, but later on it becomes a natural part of the process.

To make the learning easier, I will walk you through my daily stocks scanning. If you are more advanced trader you probably have your own Trade Ideas(TI) scanner, if not, you can use one here: https://www.Youtube.com/@STOCKSROCKS .This Youtube channel streams TI scanner every day for years now, the only downside is it has two minutes delay. But even with a two minute delay you are not going to miss many good entries. In addition to that, this channel has voice over news.

I sit down at my computer at 8:30AM and the first thing I see are my scanners. In the pre-market Gappers scanner is the most important one. It shows which stocks have Gapped up the most since the last trading section as you can see in the *Image C1*.

DAY TRADING

Image C1

Symbol	Price ($)	Gap (%)	Flt (Shr)	Vol Today (Shr)	Vol 5 Min (%)	Earn Date (Dys)
BIOC	1.39	65.4	1,464,500	5,095,245	337,021.4	-18.25
AGBA	0.9445	33.2		6,275,322	790.8	-19.25
IMPL	0.5000	30.9	7,739,830	3,226,367	559.6	-14.75
ELUT	1.75	22.9	6,044,450	601,067	10,416.8	-18.25
VERB	2.04	22.2	4,059,200	1,911,079	29.1	-18.25
RNLX	2.84	12.7		6,103	879.0	36.25
BFRG	3.23	11.4	1,281,130	75,113	219.6	-18.25
SWBI	11.70	11.3	45.02M	15,023	6.2	-0.25
OKYO	2.15	10.8	25.52M	32,611	43.3	-17.75
EOSE	3.10	10.3	121.52M	187,606	0.9	-18.25
PSTV	3.27	10.1	2,485,230	1,707,339	23,422.4	-18.25
ONFO	1.29	9.3	3,010,630	163,146	771.3	-18.75
LVO	1.78	8.5	85.15M	41,137	51.9	-20.75
SPRB	2.42	8.5	19.38M	14,817	0.2	-18.25
BON	0.6550	8.3	7,476,340	20,019	0.0	-17.75
BGLC	1.12	7.7	6,552,700	1,061,583	60.7	
EDBL	0.9498	6.7	2,260,270	39,540	2.2	-20.75
IBRX	1.19	6.1	108.72M	24,543	4.0	-22.25
SMAR	42.90	6.3	127.40M	5,948	0.1	-0.25
FNGR	6.47	5.9	26.83M	89,700	12.5	24.25
XERS	2.26	5.6	128.33M	8,186	0.0	-22.75
LSDI	0.5600	-5.1	11.26M	61,259	1.1	
DOCN	25.20	-5.2	53.17M	27,722	6.6	41.75

The following requirements for the momentums stocks are:

- Float - $500k - $8million;
  There is a huge misconception in trading communities regarding low float stocks. Yes, they are more volatile, but at the same time they make bigger moves and we want to be part of these moves. Little higher risk, but way higher reward. The beauty of low float stocks is that when they are moving fast, it's easy to read their price action. Where large float stocks move like whales and take time to make a move, most of the time shaking out stops before changing the direction. That's why I never trade AAPL, MSFT, TSLA, NVDA or any other large cap stock. Somedays you will even see a stock with a float of 1 million having 40 millions shares volume. It means that float would have been cycled 40 times and there's nothing wrong with it. And lastly, "someone can just buy or drop a huge

amount of shares" and flush the price. Same happens with the large float stocks. And if you are really afraid of these flushes don't forget if the price drops too fast, it gets halted. Personally, I have never had any issues regarding this common concern.

- Price - $1 - $7;
  Low priced stocks can make bigger moves. From $1 to $2 is a 100% gain which can happen within minutes. You will never see such gains on high priced stocks.

- Volume - High (minimum 500,000)
  When I look at the scanner, I look at the stocks with the highest volume because they can have the cleanest price action. Looking at the *Image C1*, if we'd remove 1st, 2nd and 3rd stocks, anything above 1 million volume would look high and would have cleaner price action than any other stock with lower volume

- Gap UP - At least +10%.
  The Gap % is least important, sometimes stocks with 5% Gap Up will provide better trading opportunities than the ones with 150%.

Following what is written above, we would pick these four stocks: BIOC, VERB, PSTV, BGLC. These four would be the only stocks that I would look at that moment.

I would add AGBA to my second screen because it's gapping up and has a lot of volume (I know it doesn't show the float). I would keep an eye once it gets over $1 and see how the price moves. In addition to that, I would add ELUT to my second screen because it has all criterias except volume which can come in at any time.

Going back to our four stocks (BIOC, VERB, PSTV and BGLC) , I would go through every single step for each one of them:

Step 1 - Price Action on 1 min and 5 min charts
The stock has to be trading in a clean price action. We have already defined what the price action is and now let's look at a couple of examples so we would be able to recognise what clean price action is.

Our first example is a clean price action which can be defined by large candles moving up or down, short wicks to the both sides, up and down, no gaps between the candles, as shown in the (*Image C2*).

Image C2

The next example is a not clean price action because the price action is really wicky. Trading during such conditions is extremely hard because the price moves so much and the risk is usually not worth the reward. We try to avoid such candles as much as we can.

Image C3

In the last example you can see a not clean price action. I never trade such action and the only reason why it looks like that is the lack of volume (*Image C4*).

Image C4

If the stock doesn't have a clean price action like in the *Image C2* or *Image C3*, I would discard it right away or move it to my second screen to keep an eye on it in case the price action gets better.

You might hear that some people trade only one or two tickers and that's it. Mostly these stocks are APPL, AMZN, TSLA, PLTR or AMD. These stocks have a lot of volume every day, but they have massive floats which makes them impossible for momentum trading. In addition to that, most of the large float stocks follow SPY index. There are certain days when these stocks have news and they are moving independently from the SPY, but most of the time they are following it. Trading momentum we never get stuck with the same stocks. We go where the volume and clean price action is.

Step 2 - Moving Averages on Daily chart
I check if the price is above these Moving Averages on **Daily chart**:

- Above 9 Simple Moving Average;
- Above 20 Simple Moving Average;
- Above 50 Simple Moving Average;
- Above 100 Simple Moving Average;
- Above 200 Simple Moving Average.

Image C5

DAY TRADING

As you can see in the (*Image C5*) the price is trading under the moving averages which would be an indication for me not to trade that stock. If you are an inexperienced trader I highly suggest trading only when the price is above all of these moving averages. If you have more experience, trading between these averages is still a possibility, but you need to be more cautious.

As in the (*Image C5*), the stock met all of my requirements except trading above all moving averages. I did trade this stock, but I waited until the price went above the Pink Moving average and I traded it until it reached the Orange Moving Average.

Image C6

In the (*Image C6*) you can see that the price is between 100 SMA and 50 SMA, however I would never trade a stock with such a daily price action. The reason is - the last candle, which is still forming, is trading lower than the highs of the two previous days. For me this means that there will be a lot of resistance and the price movement will be irregular and hard to read. I would only look at this stock if the price would go above $0.31 and then I would know there is no recent resistance ahead. If you look at the first Big Green candle that started the uptrend it had no recent resistance.

In the *(Image C7)* price is trading above all moving averages on the daily chart which is great, however I would wait until the price would move above the recent resistance (blue line). Once the price is above that blue line, my hand would be on the trigger and eyes on Level 2.

Image C7

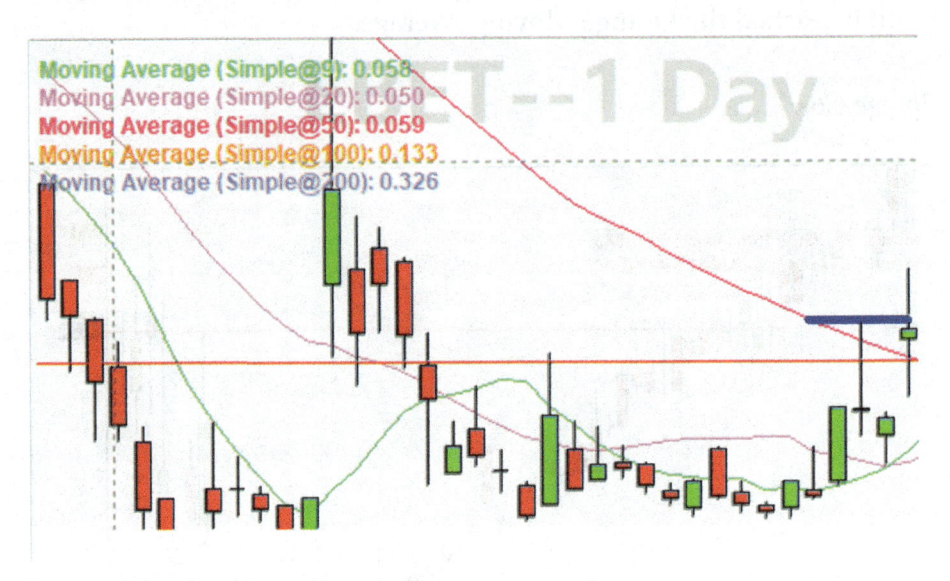

Step 3 - Level 2 is thick enough, but not too thick
To simply explain - on Level 2 BIDs and ASKs should have enough orders at every price level. In the *(Image C8)* below you can see that there are no price gaps between price levels. Level 2 looking like this is the best option to have.

Image C8

BID	SIZE	ASK	SIZE
1.08	47	1.09	16
1.08	41	1.09	14
1.08	41	1.09	10
1.08	38	1.09	10
1.08	38	1.09	5
1.08	38	1.09	5
1.08	7	1.10	45
1.08	4	1.10	2
1.08	2	1.10	2
1.07	36	1.10	1
1.06	32	1.11	60
1.05	25	1.12	48

Too thick Level 2 is when at every price level we have huge standing orders on both sides and because these massive orders are on every price level the price is not able to move fast to create trading opportunities (*Image C9*).

Image C9

BID	SIZE	ASK	SIZE
20.54	151	20.55	455
20.54	117	20.55	455
20.54	100	20.55	439
20.54	96	20.55	316
20.54	91	20.55	242
20.54	91	20.55	212
20.54	56	20.55	117
20.54	11	20.55	114
20.54	1	20.55	111
20.53	269	20.55	85
20.53	127	20.55	76
20.53	108	20.55	56

Too thin Level 2 is when the price levels are scattered and increasing/decreasing by more than $0.01-0.02. We stay away from this thin Level 2 because the price movement is unpredictable and the price can easily jump up or down very fast *(Image C10)*.

Image C10

BID	SIZE	ASK	SIZE
5.04	3	5.10	34
5.04	2	5.15	10
5.02	5	5.15	6
5.02	0	5.15	1
5.01	1	5.25	0
5.00	1	5.32	1
5.00	1	5.32	1
4.89	1	5.34	1
4.87	0	5.39	0
4.86	0	5.40	1
4.83	6		
4.52	6		

If you are still new to the trading, I highly suggest avoiding any stock that has more than $0.01-$0.02 gaps between price levels. If you are more experienced and can manage your risk, you can trade those thinner Level 2s without any problems.

At the beginning it might take you a while to understand which Level 2 is good for trading or if the price action is clean enough. There will be days where you will see that thick or thin Level 2 has a readable price action and trade it.

As you can see my stock selection process is pretty fast and usually takes 2-3 minutes of my time to go through the gappers scanner. There are days when I look at 4-5 stocks at the same time and there are some days when I watch only 1-2 stocks. But do not underestimate its simplicity since it provides you all required information to assess if the stocks are suitable for momentum trading or not.

IMPORTANT. New traders should follow these parameters and do not trade any stocks that don't have all required criteria, Once you get more knowledge, you will start noticing that you can have some deviation from the original parameters. You will see that one day a stock with 30 million float is moving as a momentum stock, or the stock which is priced $0.60 is moving as a momentum stock. With more experience your spectrum of tradable stocks will grow, however you need to be careful because sometimes you can go too far.

CHAPTER 5
FINDING AN UPTREND

Once I choose from the scanner which stocks I am going to check, I need to see if they are uptrending. I look at its 5 minute chart and it needs to fulfil these four criteria, if at least one of them is missing, I am not going to trade it and wait until it fulfils all four criteria:

1. Price is above 9 Exponential Moving Average on 5 min chart;
2. Price is above 20 Exponential Moving Average on 5 min chart;
3. Price is above Volume Weighted Average Price on 5 min chart;
4. Price is close to the High of Day.

First three are pretty easy to distinguish, the last one is more subjective. I can't tell you how much % of the retracement or how many points pullback still counts as close to the High of the Day. With time you will easily notice these charts, but for starters you can follow this rule - if the price is about to break the High of the Day or price broke High of the Day and it's on its first pull back. By following this simple rule, you will always be fulfilling the fourth criteria.

After that, I will check if the price is uptrending on the 5 min chart. And you check it simply by looking at the candles:

- They are making higher highs;

- They are making higher lows;
- They are green;

Candle size doesn't matter. You don't need to draw any channels or trendlines, you just look at higher highs and higher lows. It doesn't have to be a perfect pattern. Each of those patterns in *(Image D1)* are beautiful in their own way and provide many great trading opportunities.

Image D1

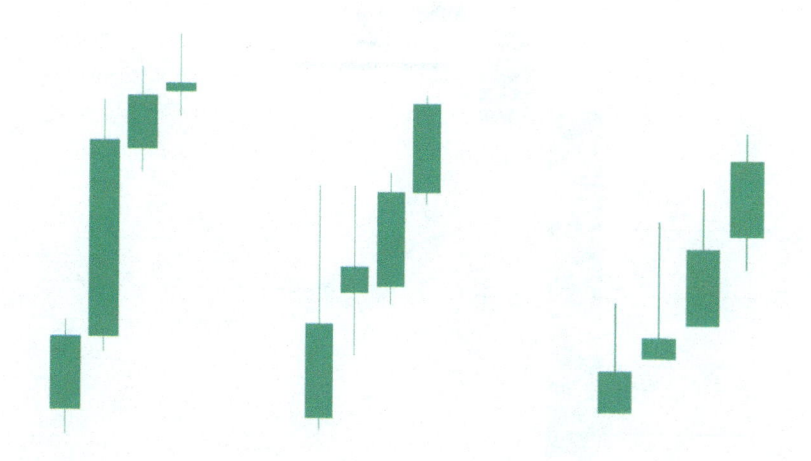

Any trade within these candles would be considered as a good trade. And yes, sometimes you might enter at the top of the candle and the price could go down, but we will get into it later in Level 2 chapter and how to reduce the chances of getting caught being in the move down.

Uptrend, but the price is pulling back
As always, the 5 minutes chart has to fulfil the four criteria that I mentioned before.

Let's say we have an uptrend, higher highs and higher lows, green candles, everything is great. Once any candle makes a lower low or closes as a red candle, I consider it as the start of the pullback. Sometimes it can be just a minor pullback and the price starts surging up right away, but we need to be more cautious because it signals weakness in the price action. But to be on the safe side, I look at it as the start of the pullback and avoid putting trades on.

Image D2

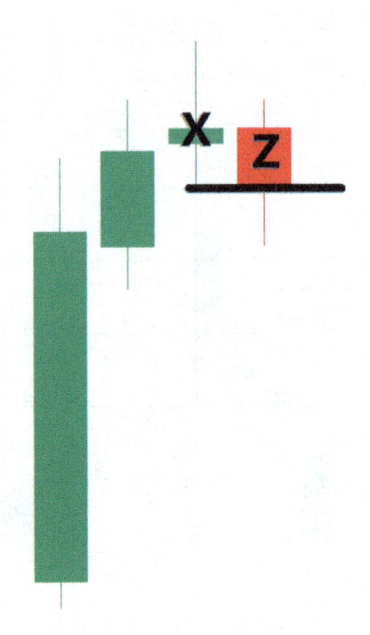

As you can see in the (*Image D2*), we have 2 candles, one named X and another named Z. The black line is the Low price of the X candle. Once the Z candle's price broke that line, the pullback started. There are many variations of candles that start the pull back. Here is an example of a green candle that I would consider as a start of the pullback in (*Image D3*).

Image D3

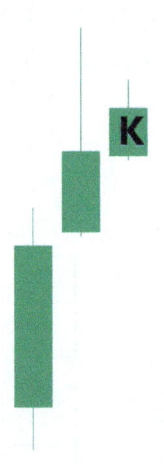

Even though candle K is green in *(Image D3)*, it has a lower high which would tell me that the price action is exhausting and losing its momentum and a pullback is incoming.

Again, if any of the candles don't have these parameters, I consider it as the start of the pull back and avoid placing any trades.

- They are making higher highs;
- They are making higher lows;
- They are green.

Pullbacks come in many different shapes, sizes and lengths. Some may last a few minutes, some might last hours and some might be that price is actually down trending.

I consider a healthy pullback on 5 minute charts until it comes back to 9 EMA. Anything more than that reduces the momentum of the price action and I would trade that stock again only if it would go back close to the High of the Day or hit my scanners.

My rule during the pullback is always to look for a trade once the first candle makes a higher high. Usually I wait for 2-3 candles, which is 10-15 minutes. If it doesn't happen, I will start looking for other stocks to trade. I will enter trade on the first 5 min higher highs only if the Level 2 confirms it.

Image D4

As you can see on the left side of the *(Image D4)*, that's how a perfect price action looks like. Whenever the candle M broke the high of the P candle, the new uptrend started.

But if we look to the right side of the *(Image D4)*, we can see that the C candle broke the high of the R candle, turned around and went down. That's why placing trades based only on charts is so disadvantageous. It all depends on what Level 2 is showing.

More cautious approach would be to wait until the price comes back to the high of the day and look for the trade there *(Image D5)*.

Image D5

When the price action on the 5 minute chart is validating all of my required parameters above moving averages, higher highs etc.). I will look at the 1 minute chart to find the entry price for my trade. To make it clear, I will look for the entry price only, but I will not enter the trade yet.

Here is a perfect example of a 1 minute pullback (*Image D6*).

Image D6

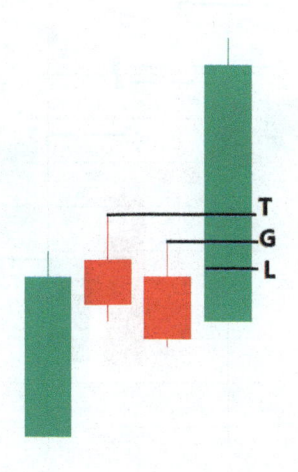

T - Entry price would be the High of the Day on 1 minute chart;
G - Entry price would be the break of the previous candle high on 1 minute chart;
L - Early entry price based only on Level 2;

No matter which trade I would be taking, all of them would need to be confirmed by Level 2. T and G trades are more safe, but still need to be validated by Level 2. Trade L is based on how the price has been moving and Level 2, but for this one you need to have a lot of experience. All you need to understand for this moment is how to find these entry prices on the 1 minute chart.

The Color of the candles on 1 minute pull back doesn't matter. All we look for is the previous candle high or High of the day.

But as you know, whenever we trade, we never get these perfect patterns. It always looks like a swamp monster with 8 legs. In *(Image D7)* you can see an example of where I would have looked for entry prices.

Image D7

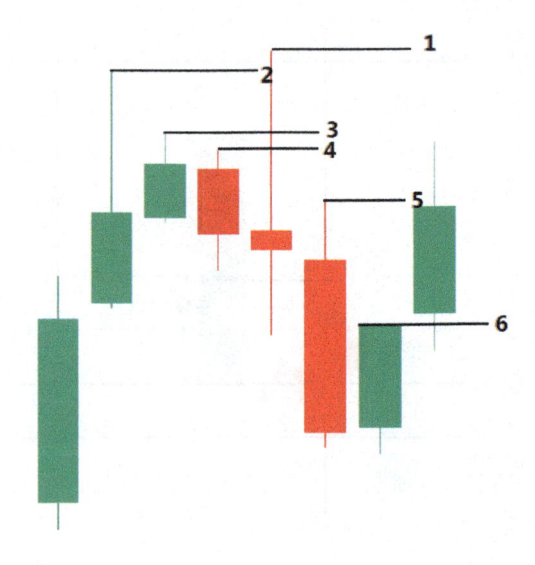

That is the reason why we never trade based only on charts, we only look for the entry price in them. It is very easy to get caught in false breakouts and then get flushed down. It happens to everyone and it's part of the trading, but we will minimise it to protect your money later while studying Level 2. Most important thing from the 1 minute chart is to be able to find the entry price.

This is all you need to know from 1 minute and 5 minute charts. Just make sure the 5 minute charts have all of the required parameters and find the entry prices on the 1 minute chart. And every day I find many opportunities to trade this strategy.

CHAPTER 6
WHO IS MOVING THE PRICE?

Before we start analysing Level 2 we need to understand who is moving the price at certain moments. We can never be 100% sure, but we can learn to notice when short sellers are entering or when the buyers are getting exhausted. This takes time to learn this and you can do it only by watching Level 2 when the price comes to certain levels.

Image E1

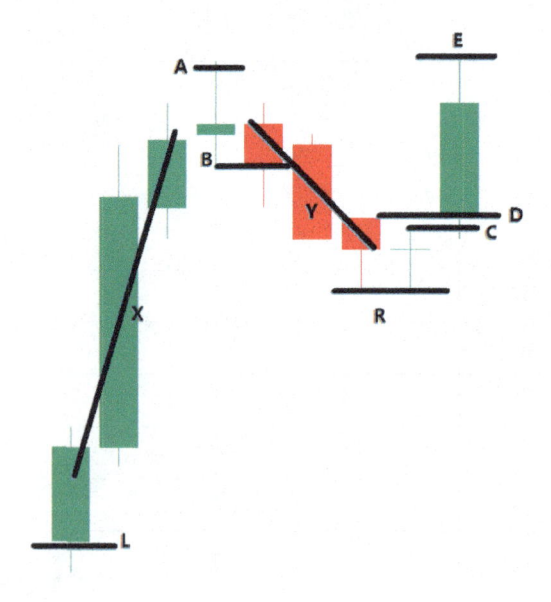

L - Price level where the uptrend move started. For training purposes we will say that this level was the previous High of the Day.

X - Price is rising as more and more buyers are stepping in. You still get wicks at the top of the candles because there are people who short at that point and there are people who sell to take their profits because they entered earlier.

A - Is the price area where the buyers get exhausted which means there is not enough demand or buying power to push the price further. Based on Level 2 and price not being able to make a higher high, some short sellers would enter positions with the stop loss above or even at the peak of the last move, at this point would be A. So short sellers are shorting and people who had Long positions are starting to cover by selling, which pushes the price even further down.

B - Is a price area where many people see a change of the current trend. The time frame does not matter, it can be 1 minute or 4 hour candle, it's the same rule that applies to all time frames. At point B the first red candle makes a Lower Low which is a confirmation to many traders that it is time to cover your long positions by selling and even more short sellers are coming in since they have a confirmation that the trend has changed.

Y - We have a little downtrend or since it's after a huge move up - a pull back. During the pull back most of the Longs are still covering (closing) their positions and more short sellers are joining the move. This pull back is natural and healthy for any type of stock. So the price keeps dropping until point R.

R - This is the price area, most of the time it's 9 EMA or 20 EMA on 1 minute or 5 minute charts. It doesn't have to be any of the moving averages, it can be a full number, half number or just any random price number. The point is that we can see the price can't break that level and go any lower. We don't know the reason why and we don't look for it because we will never know. It can be an institution buying or a hedge fund, we will never know. Because the price can't break down trough R area and more buyers are starting to notice it and enter their long positions which starts to push price higher. Short Sellers, who entered at point A see the same, the price can't push down any further, they start closing their positions (buying) which pushes the price up even more.

C - First confirmation, Higher High, that the current trend has changed and it's uptrending. It's a signal to many short sellers to cover their position (buy) and a signal to many traders to enter their Long positions.

D - The same as C, second confirmation, second Higher High, and price is going to skyrocket in a matter of seconds since millions of people know this pattern and wait for confirmation to enter their long traders. And when the price pushes higher it takes out remaining short sellers and their stops, which makes them automatically help the move go higher.

E - The High of the Day, the area where short sellers will enter and buyers will enter at the same time. The side which loses will have price pushed in their way and stops will be taken out. If sellers win - people who went long will have their stops activated or they will manually exit the trade by selling and adding more momentum to the *downside*. If buyers win - people who went short will have their stops activated or they will manually exit the trade by buying and adding more momentum to the *upside*.

After trading for a long time this knowledge becomes a natural process and you don't think about it. It's always in the back of your head and once you see a lower low or a higher high it activates and reminds you how to perceive the market. Now, I understand that the chart in *(Image E1)* is a perfect graph and this does not happen all the time, but I want you to understand who is pushing the price so you would have a better understanding of the market and take advantage of it.

If you look at this chart *(Image E2)*, you will see that it's impossible to say exactly when the longs are entering or shorts are selling. That's why momentum strategy works only on certain stocks with high volume and some volatility. Some of you might wonder how you can know when the price has reached its peak and the answer is Level 2.

Image E2

During the morning, I wasn't focused on this stock *(Image E2)*, but because it had high volume, I kept it on my second screen. After 10 minutes I looked at it and saw that it became from untradeable stock to tradeable because more volume came in and the moves started to look more clear. I moved this stock back to my main screen because of the cleaner price action (*Image E3*). Once the price broke $1.32 which was the High of the Day, many people got alert on their scanners and joined the move. And because more people are participating in the move, the cleaner the price is and it's more liquid which makes it easier to enter and exit trades.

Image E3

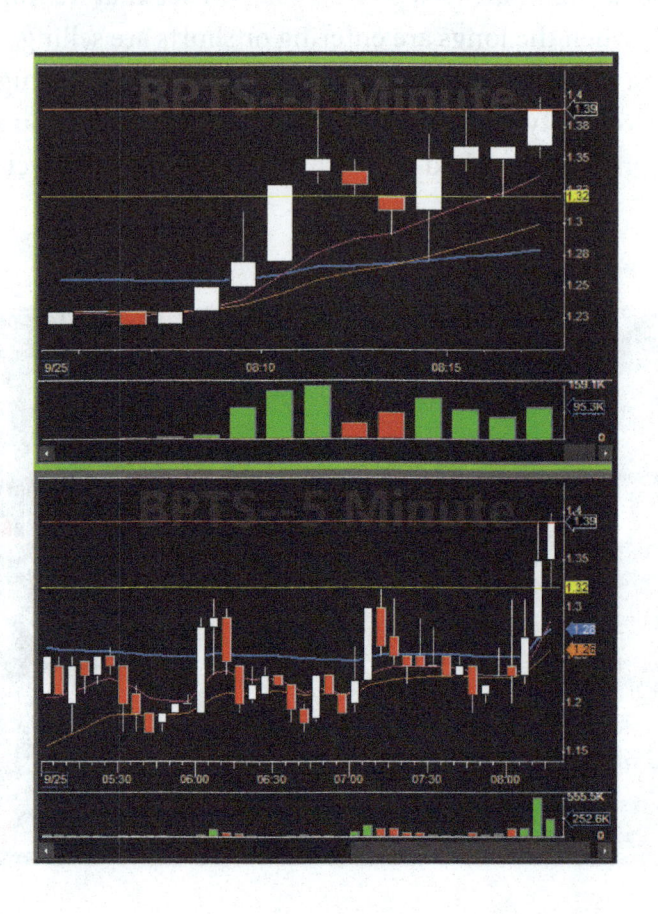

Again, to make sure you understand, momentum trading only works on the stocks that have all required parameters. If you try to use this strategy on a low volume stock or large cap stock, it will never work. That's why choosing the right stock is as important as putting a trade on.

CHAPTER 7
HOW TO READ LEVEL 2

There is not much information about Level 2 and most of the time you can find people saying that the understanding of it comes with experience and it is true. It is really hard to explain how Level 2 works because it is constantly moving and, as you know, you can't put videos into the books. I will do my best to explain how I see Level 2 and how I use it for my trading. There are many ways to interpret it and if you disagree with me, I am fine with that because you need to find what works for you. My goal is to bring your understanding of Level 2 to a certain point where you would be able to enter and exit trades.

Here in *(Image F1)* you can see a clean example of how Level 2 looks like. And most important things for us are BID and ASK prices and their sizes.

Image F1

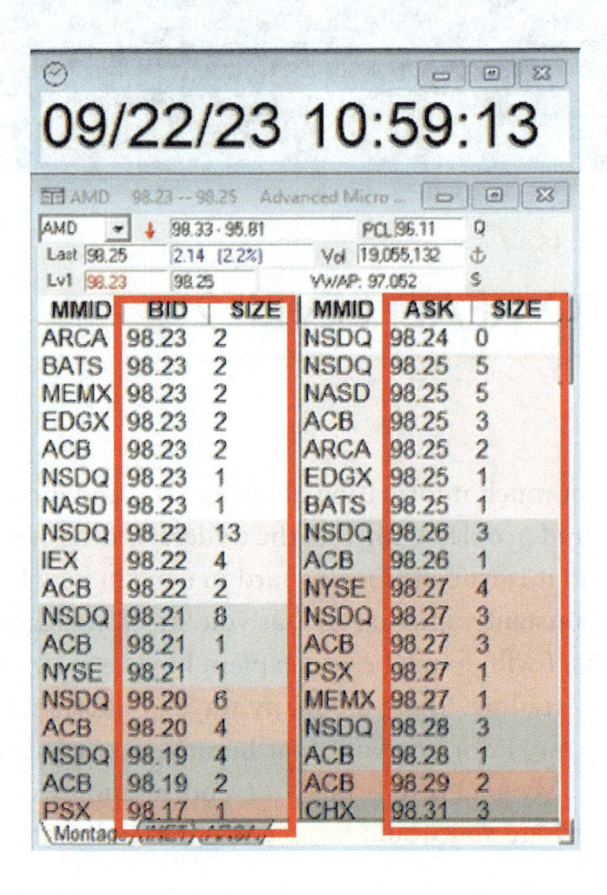

MMID	BID	SIZE	MMID	ASK	SIZE
ARCA	98.23	2	NSDQ	98.24	0
BATS	98.23	2	NSDQ	98.25	5
MEMX	98.23	2	NASD	98.25	5
EDGX	98.23	2	ACB	98.25	3
ACB	98.23	2	ARCA	98.25	2
NSDQ	98.23	1	EDGX	98.25	1
NASD	98.23	1	BATS	98.25	1
NSDQ	98.22	13	NSDQ	98.26	3
IEX	98.22	4	ACB	98.26	1
ACB	98.22	2	NYSE	98.27	4
NSDQ	98.21	8	NSDQ	98.27	3
ACB	98.21	1	ACB	98.27	3
NYSE	98.21	1	PSX	98.27	1
NSDQ	98.20	6	MEMX	98.27	1
ACB	98.20	4	NSDQ	98.28	3
NSDQ	98.19	4	ACB	98.28	1
ACB	98.19	2	ACB	98.29	2
PSX	98.17	1	CHX	98.31	3

BID is showing at what prices buyers are willing to buy stocks.

ASK is showing at what prices sellers are willing to sell their stocks.

It's simple like that. We do not need to dig deeper where Short Sellers are on the BID trying to cover their positions or maybe Longs are trying to cover their positions. Since we can't know, we perceive it as it is.

BID = BUYERS
ASK = SELLERS

The number of the size on Level 2

On most trading platforms you will see Level 2 like this and the sizes will be written in hundreds.

Image F2

BID	SIZE	ASK	SIZE
1.02	600	1.03	400
1.01	800	1.04	700
1.00	500	1.05	300

I have changed it on my platform to show numbers in Lots:

1 Lot = 100 shares.

And if there are under 100 shares on the Level 2 it will be showing zero which means there are less than hundred shares on each price level.

Image F3

BID	SIZE	ASK	SIZE
1.02	0	1.03	0

It is up to every trader individually to find what his preferences are, but I try to shave off as much time as possible to perceive information faster. When I perceive Level 2, all I need to think is about single or double digits, otherwise I would need to think in hundreds which would take more time. When I will be saying that I am buying or selling one share, it means that I am talking in Lots.

DAY TRADING

For the learning process, we will use my simplified Level 2 which will help to understand and display the movement of the price (*Image F4*).

Image F4

BID	SIZE	ASK	SIZE
1.02	1	1.03	1
1.01	1	1.04	1
1.00	1	1.05	1

As you can see, our Level 2 (*Image F4*) is pretty simple and already provides a lot of information. It shows the spread which is $0.01 ($1.03 - $1.02), it shows how thinly or thickly the stock is traded, at the moment it's ok, since it has sellers and buyers and every price level. And the size shows how fast the price can change (will explain more about it later).

Now, let's imagine that my neighbour told me that the price of this stock will go to $10 in a week. So I went and bought 2 shares. And because I want them right now, I don't place a LIMIT order and wait until the price comes to fill my order. I buy it on the ASK as a MARKET order (*Image F5*).

Image F5

BID	SIZE	ASK	SIZE
1.02	1	1.03	1
1.01	1	1.04	1
1.00	1	1.05	1

DAY TRADING

I buy and pay $1.03 for one share and I pay $1.04 for the second share *(Image F5)*. By doing that, these 2 orders of $1.03 and $1.04 on Level 2 will get removed because they got filled by me buying them. So the Level 2 price levels on the ASK move up *(Image F6)*.

Image F6

BID	SIZE	ASK	SIZE
1.02	1	1.05	1
1.01	1	1.06	1
1.00	1	1.07	1

Now we have BID at $1.02 and ASK at $1.05 which makes the spread $0.03 cents. If you buy a share at $1.05, you would be instantly down $0.03 because the highest current buyer on the BID is $1.02.

What is going to happen next:

1) Someone will notice that I bought shares on the ASK price and will think "Oh, it seems the price is going up, but I don't want to rush. I will place 2 orders to buy 1 share each: one at $1.03 and one at $1.04

Image F7

BID	SIZE	ASK	SIZE
1.04	1	1.05	1
1.03	1	1.06	1
1.02	1	1.07	1

DAY TRADING

Again, we have a Level 2 with a price spread of $0.01, but the price on our chart moved up because the BID and ASK is $1.04 and $1.05 (*Image F7*) where before it was $1.02 and $1.03 (*Image F4*).

2) Someone will notice that I bought shares on the ASK price and will think "Oh, it seems someone is buying at $1.03 and $1.04, since I bought shares at $0.90 I will reduce my risk and place 2 shares to sell at $1.03 and $1.04 accordingly (*Image F8*).

Image F8

BID	SIZE	ASK	SIZE
1.02	1	1.03	1
1.01	1	1.04	1
1.00	1	1.05	1

We are back where we started with BID $1.02, ASK $1.03 and $0.01 spread.

There are many variations of what could happen, but let's keep it simple for now so we can have a better understanding of how the price is moving. Just to know, as simple as it looks, this price movement is the cornerstone of placing trades and trading using Level 2.

Here is an example how would it look like for the price to go down:

We have the same starting Level 2. BID at $1.02 and ASK at $1.03 with a spread of $0.01 (*Image F9*).

Image F9

BID	SIZE	ASK	SIZE
1.02	1	1.03	1
1.01	1	1.04	1
1.00	1	1.05	1

Let's say I bought 2 shares when the price was $0.80 and now I believe that anything above $1.00 is a great price to cover and sell my position of 2 shares. So I sell into the BID for $1.02 for 1 share and $1.01 for another 1 (*Image F10*).

Image F10

BID	SIZE	ASK	SIZE
1.02	1	1.03	1
1.01	1	1.04	1
1.00	1	1.05	1

So I take out the two highest price orders standing on the BID and the Level 2 would look like this (*Image F11*).

Image F11

BID	SIZE	ASK	SIZE
1.00	1	1.03	1
0.99	1	1.04	1
0.98	1	1.05	1

Now someone who bought the stock at price $0.75 sees that BIDs above $1 are getting filled, he thinks he will be able to exit at $1.01 and $1.02 as well, so he places these orders as LIMIT ORDERS on the ASK. And then we have the Level 2 like this (*Image F12*).

Image F12

BID	SIZE	ASK	SIZE
1.00	1	1.01	1
0.99	1	1.02	1
0.98	1	1.03	1

We have the BID at $1.00, the ASK at $1.01 and the spread of $0.01, but the price on the chart will go down because the price levels of the BID and ASK went down.

It will not be easy to read the Level 2 at the beginning because most of the time prices will be jumping up and down all the time. The sizes will be changing, orders will appear or disappear from nowhere, but slowly you will start noticing when the ASK gets bought, the price moves up or when the BID gets filled the price goes down.

CHAPTER 8
MOMENTUM ENTRIES BASED ON LEVEL 2

Placing trades is the most complicated part of the trading. You have to see not the 1 minute, 5 minute and Daily charts at the same time, but follow and feel what is going on on Level 2 and Time & Sales.

Since I am trading Momentum strategy only when the price rises it is easier to focus on Level 2 and look for signals indicating that the price will surge up.

To make it more visual, I will use an analogy:

BIDs - are our defence line
ASKs - are our offence line

In order for the price to go up, BIDs and ASKs have to work together and I will show you how to perceive this information better.

Here we have our Level 2 *(Image G1)*.

Image G1

BID	SIZE	ASK	SIZE
1.02	1	1.03	1
1.01	1	1.04	1
1.00	1	1.05	1

Our ASK offence line has pushed the prices further and we have Level 2 looking like this (*Image G2*).

Image G2

BID	SIZE	ASK	SIZE
1.02	1	1.05	1
1.01	1	1.06	1
1.00	1	1.07	1

For the price to go up, our defence line has to step up and push higher as well (*Image G3*).

Image G3

BID	SIZE	ASK	SIZE
1.04	1	1.05	1
1.03	1	1.06	1
1.02	1	1.07	1

If the BIDs don't push the price higher, there might be new orders appearing on ASK at $1.02 and $1.03 which would make the price go back to where it was. Most of the times when the ASK offence line pushes the price, but BIDs defence line stays the same, you can expect the price to go back down very fast and even take out some of the BIDs lowering the price even more. To make it more simple, there have to be people who are willing to pay and buy on the ASK and people who are placing their buy orders on the ASK when the price is rising.

Now, let's take a different approach. Level 2 looks like this (*Image G4*)

Image G4

BID	SIZE	ASK	SIZE
1.02	1	1.03	1
1.01	1	1.04	1
1.00	1	1.05	1

Someone came and filled BID orders at $1.02 and $1.01 and now we have Level 2 looking like this (Image G5).

Image G5

BID	SIZE	ASK	SIZE
1.00	1	1.03	1
0.99	1	1.04	1
0.98	1	1.05	1

The best outcome would be if BIDs stepped up and placed orders at $1.01 and $1.02 which would bring the Level 2 to where it was before. The worst outcome would be if ASKs would step down and retreat to fill the missing gap. But there is a third outcome which would be ASKs pushing the price higher and we would have Level 2 looking like this (*Image G6*).

Image G6

BID	SIZE	ASK	SIZE
1.00	1	1.06	1
0.99	1	1.07	1
0.98	1	1.08	1

This is where the price actions get choppy and hard to read because the price fluctuates too much. It will take a few seconds for the price action to calm down and even out. After those few seconds you will see that price increased or decreased depending on how many buyers and how many sellers were there during the fluctuation.

Time & Sales

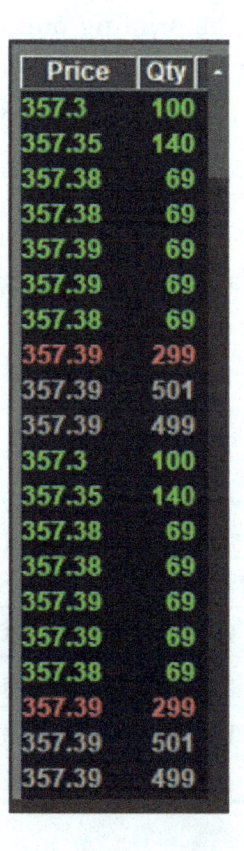

Price	Qty
357.3	100
357.35	140
357.38	69
357.38	69
357.39	69
357.39	69
357.38	69
357.39	299
357.39	501
357.39	499
357.3	100
357.35	140
357.38	69
357.38	69
357.39	69
357.39	69
357.38	69
357.39	299
357.39	501
357.39	499

Before we approach entries and exits, we need to talk about Time & Sales since it works hand in hand with Level 2.

Many of you heard that even decades of the years passed Time & Sales, or the Tape, has remained the same. Well, this is incorrect. Back in the days the volume of the trades was way lower so the Tape had been printing orders much slower than at the current day. Imagine back in the 60's the tape printing hundreds of orders every second. No one would be able to read it, the machine itself would catch a fire. Due to technology markets became accessible to millions of people and placing trades takes a few milliseconds. And when you look at the Time & Sales of the stock that is trading in large volume quantities,

DAY TRADING

like the ones we use for momentum trading, you will not be able to see much in it because it will be printing numbers too fast. Of course, if you look at the stock that trades a few thousand shares a day, its tape will be moving really slow, but because it is so illiquid there is no point trading it, at least for me.

However, we can still get some information from the Time & Sales, even if it's moving really fast. Let me show you where I apply it.

Here we have our Level 2, but this time ASK at the price $1.03 has 78 shares to sell *(Image G7)*.

Image G7

BID	SIZE	ASK	SIZE
1.02	1	1.03	78
1.01	1	1.04	1
1.00	1	1.05	1

For our offence line to push further, the first 78 shares at $1.03 have to be taken out. While at the same time, we have only 1 share on our defence line at $1.02. When I see a Level 2 like this, my first thought is the price will go down, but it has a potential to go up.

When I have a Level 2 like this, automatically I split my focus between Level 2 and Time & Sales. What I want to see is the Time & Sales printing speed increasing with more and more green prints. While at the same time I want to see the order on the ASK to get filled.

So Time & Sales speed is increasing and Level 2 starts showing the ASK being filled *(Image G8)*.

Image G8

BID	SIZE	ASK	SIZE
1.02	1	**1.03**	**63**
1.01	1	1.04	1
1.00	1	1.05	1

Time & Sales keeps printing faster and faster, and Level 2 now looks like this *(Image G9).*

Image G9

BID	SIZE	ASK	SIZE
1.02	1	**1.03**	**28**
1.01	1	1.04	1
1.00	1	1.05	1

Again, the Time & Sales are going crazy and more ASKs are getting filled and the size on the ASK at $1.03 is getting smaller and smaller *(Image G10).*

Image G10

BID	SIZE	ASK	SIZE
1.02	1	**1.03**	**9**
1.01	1	1.04	1
1.00	1	1.05	1

Now this is the most important moment for momentum trading. To understand what happened, let's analyse what has changed and what hasn't changed.

First, and most important, the ASK size at $1.03 went from 78 to 9. At the same time, the BID held its position at $1.02. This shows that there are way more aggressive buyers than sellers and the price is about to surge up. And when the price does surge up, most likely it will take out $1.04 and $1.05 because of the momentum and the price will jump even higher.

This moment when the ASKs are getting filled and the BIDs are holding the line, it is our buying signal. Before you press the BUY button, you need to see if the price level on your 1 minute chart and 5 minute chart is in the right price area. The perfect example would be this setup *(Image G11)*.

Image G11

This ABCD/Bull Flag setup with ASKs being taken out and BIDs holding the line is the best possible entry with the highest success

rate. **The speed of Time & Sales confirms that these ASKs are getting filled and not traders removing their orders from the ASK.**

We have our first entry signal and we can see how everything that we learnt so far works together. However, Time & Sales have a couple more indications that we need to know of. So let's look again at our Level 2, but this time we have a big BID (*Image G12*).

Image G12

BID	SIZE	ASK	SIZE
1.02	96	1.03	1
1.01	1	1.04	1
1.00	1	1.05	1

When I see Level 2 like this, my first thought is that the price is going to go up, but it has a chance to flush down.

Remember, BIDs are our defence line, the more the better. But once we start seeing them being filled and the size at $1.02 going from 96->78->50->24>5 signals us that there are aggressive sellers and our defence line will be pushed through in a second and the price will get flushed down. At the same time, Time & Sales speed is increasing and it's printing red numbers faster and faster which validates that these sellers are real.

So how can we use this information if we are trading only when the price is going up. There are 2 instances how seeing BIDs being taken out could help our trading.

First, let's say we entered position at $0.90, price went up and the Level 2 looks like this (*Image G13*).

Image G13

BID	SIZE	ASK	SIZE
1.02	96	1.03	1
1.01	1	1.04	1
1.00	1	1.05	1

I am in a Long position because I bought shares at $0.90. I see there is a massive size on the BID. This gives me confidence because for the price to go down, 96 BID positions have to be taken out while to go up, only 1 position has to be taken out at $1.03. **At the same time, if I see that BIDs are getting filled and the size at $1.02 is going down 96>75>49>21>4 while the speed of Time & Sales is increasing, it would be a signal for me to exit my position before the price flushes down.**

If I don't have an open position and I am looking for an entry, seeing Level 2 like this would give me some confidence because I know there is support at $1.02. And if I see the price comes to $1.02 but doesn't break it, then goes up, comes back and tries again but unsuccessfully, this would be a signal for me to enter a Long position if the price area is in accordance with price levels that I see on my 1 minute and 5 minute charts. This is our second buying signal.

There is another important indicator that Time & Sales provide - reveals hidden sellers. Easiest way to explain it is to look at our Level 2 (*Image G14*).

Image G14

BID	SIZE	ASK	SIZE
1.02	1	1.03	5
1.01	1	1.04	1
1.00	1	1.05	1

We have 5 shares for sale at $1.03 on the ASK. Now, if I come in and decide to buy these 5 shares at $1.03 the price should move up and the highest ASK should change to $1.04. So let's say I press the BUY button and I get filled (order can be seen on Time & Sales). I bought 5 shares on the ASK, but Level 2 looks exactly the same (*Image G15*).

Image G15

BID	SIZE	ASK	SIZE
1.02	1	1.03	5
1.01	1	1.04	1
1.00	1	1.05	1

As we learnt before, if the price level gets filled, it should be removed from Level 2. Now, I am angry that the price didn't move and I press another BUY button to buy 50 shares to be sure that the price moves. But the ASK stays the same and that's where the Hidden seller is. We don't know and cannot know the size of it. It might be 100 shares, it might be 10,000 shares. The possibility of the hidden sellers comes from the ability to place orders on the market and choose to show only a certain amount of shares on the Level 2. Why this is possible I don't know, but I know this happens and I need to be aware of it. **When we** notice a hidden seller, it signals us to exit the trade if we have an open position or stay away from the stock for a little bit and not place any buy orders.

As we have hidden sellers, we have hidden buyers (*Image G16*).

Image G16

BID	SIZE	ASK	SIZE
1.02	3	1.03	1
1.01	1	1.04	1
1.00	1	1.05	1

Let's say I have a position of 100 shares and I have decided to sell half of my position on the BID at $1.02. I sell 50 shares, I get filled, but the price or the size on the BID doesn't change. This indicates that there is a hidden buyer. **This signals to us that we have support to this price level and if it doesn't get pushed through, we will be able to use it as our stop if the price moves higher.** (*Image G16*)

Very important to know that we do not check ourselves by placing orders if there are hidden sellers or buyers on Level 2. We have to spot them by using Level 2 and Time & Sales. Let the other traders do the job for us and we will use this information to our advantage. Let's look at our previous example of the large size on the ASK at $1.03 (*Image G17*).

Image G17

BID	SIZE	ASK	SIZE
1.02	1	1.03	90
1.01	1	1.04	1
1.00	1	1.05	1

As before, we see the size at $1.03 starts dropping because these orders are getting filled. The size goes 90>76>52>44>23, the Time and Sales speed is increasing and increasing and we are thinking that the price is going to surge any second now. But an anomaly appears - the size at $1.03 stays 23. The Time & Sales is going crazy, printing hundreds of green orders every second, but the size on Level 2 is staying the same and the price is not moving. **This signals to us that there is a hidden seller**.

What is more, there don't need to be any huge numbers that are out of ordinary to have hidden sellers or buyers. The chart below can have hidden buyers and sellers and it's up to us to find them using Level 2 and Time & Sales. (*Image G18*)

Image G18

BID	SIZE	ASK	SIZE
1.02	6	1.03	4
1.01	8	1.04	7
1.00	5	1.05	3

Hidden sellers and buyers are common in day trading especially when trading momentum strategy and high volume stocks. Again, you need to be aware of them and act accordingly.

I hope with this chapter I managed to explain to you how to use Level 2 and Time & Sales together to find information and use it for our trading. There are a couple more points to explain because some of you are already wondering about some details.

The colours of the prints on the Time & Sales

Many traders interpret Time & Sales in many different ways. And you should do the same until you find what works for you. For me, personally, the speed of Time & Sales is more important than the colour of the prints or the sizes that are printed. But it doesn't mean that I don't take the colours of the prints into account. If I am looking at the Level 2 and Time & Sales at the price break out point, I passively see the colours of the prints because I look at the speed of the Time & Sales. And of course, seeing more green prints gives me more confidence.

Here is another great example of the price movement on Level 2 and how we can read it. Firstly, let's see how Level 2 looks (*Image G20*).

Image G20

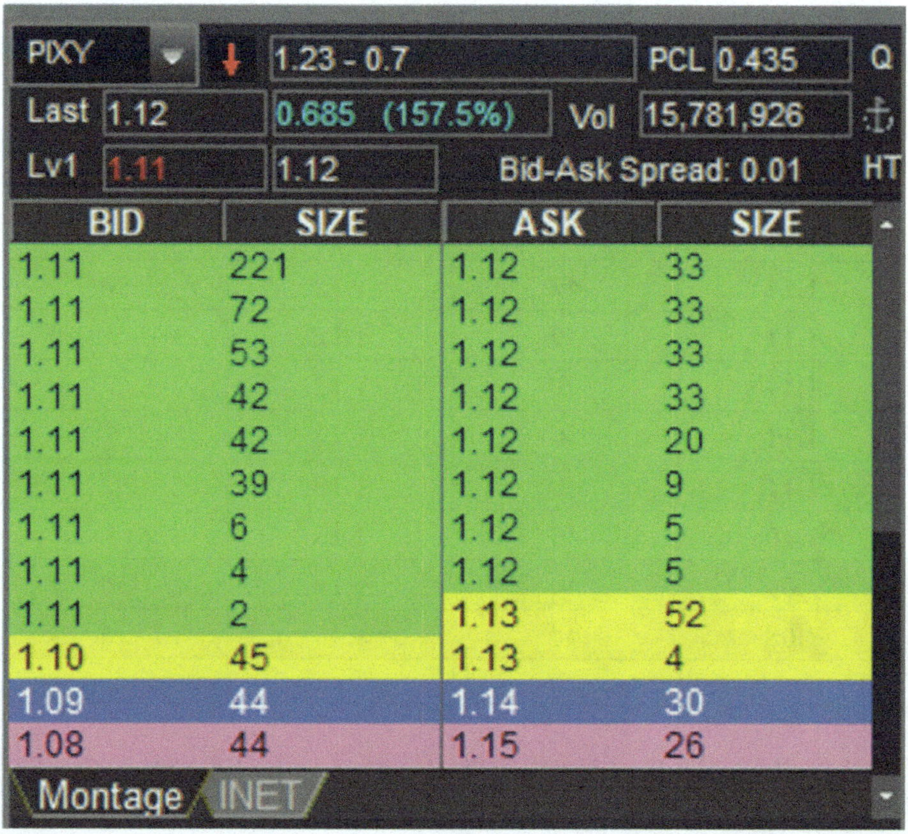

Now, let's turn this Level 2 into my homemade Level 2 (Image G21).

Image G21

BID	SIZE	ASK	SIZE
1.11	221	1.12	33
1.11	72	1.12	33
1.11	53	1.12	33
1.11	42	1.12	33
1.11	42	1.12	20
1.11	39	1.12	9
1.11	6	1.12	5
1.11	4	1.12	5
1.11	2	1.13	52
1.10	45	1.13	4
1.09	44	1.14	30
1.08	44	1.15	26

We have two identical Level 2's, just with a little different looks. For this example we will be trading in perfect conditions, which means no hidden sellers and all placed orders at every price level are real.

This time, we will focus more on the amount of the green colour on the BID side and the ASK side. When ASKs are pushing the price the Green area on the right size will shrink (*Image G23*).

Image G22

BID	SIZE	ASK	SIZE
1.11	265	1.12	27
1.11	56	1.12	49
1.11	48	1.12	52
1.11	36	1.12	16
1.11	15	1.13	20
1.11	12	1.13	9
1.11	6	1.13	5
1.11	4	1.13	5
1.11	2	1.13	52
1.10	45	1.13	4
1.09	44	1.14	30
1.08	44	1.15	26

I have changed the sizes a little bit to make it look like it actually moved. The reason we are not paying attention to the sizes this time is because the sizes on BID and ASK are so big we couldn't be able to count and compare them every second. Let's keep going and this is how Level 2 looks like after another 5 seconds (*Image G23*).

Image G23

BID	SIZE	ASK	SIZE
1.11	112	1.12	86
1.11	2	1.13	13
1.11	16	1.13	49
1.11	28	1.13	2
1.11	15	1.13	20
1.11	12	1.13	9
1.11	6	1.13	5
1.11	4	1.13	5
1.11	2	1.13	52
1.10	45	1.13	4
1.09	44	1.14	30
1.08	44	1.15	26

We have one green price level left on the ASK, the rest have been filled. **This is another signal for us to enter the trade only if the chart says that this is the right price level.** It will be even better if we wait until we see the size on the ASK at $1.12 starts dropping down 85>69>45>32>20 and we hit our buy button. Of course, this does not mean that the price will go higher every time, there might be another person who places an ASK order at $1.12 with the size of 10.000 shares.

What is more, because many traders look at such break outs, they have their fingers ready on the buy button as you do and whenever you have one green price level left on the ASK and the size is decreasing, everyone will start pulling their triggers. And because of such momentum the price can go to $1.13, $1.14 or even higher, depending on how many people participated in that move.

As we are extracting information from the ASKs, we can do the same with the BIDs. Now let's say I have entered a position with 100 shares at $1.09. The Level 2 is currently looking like this (*Image G24*).

Image G24

BID	SIZE	ASK	SIZE
1.11	265	1.12	27
1.11	56	1.12	49
1.11	48	1.12	52
1.11	36	1.12	16
1.11	15	1.13	20
1.11	12	1.13	9
1.11	6	1.13	5
1.11	4	1.13	5
1.11	2	1.13	52
1.10	45	1.13	4
1.09	44	1.14	30
1.08	44	1.15	26

We can see that the Green area on the BID is larger than the one on the ASK, which is a good support signal. We can kind of see that there are more Green orders (sizes in total) on the BID than the ASK, which is another good support signal. We gain confidence and we know that if the price will come back to $1.11 it will provide good support.

DAY TRADING

Few seconds later we see Level 2 like this (*Image G25*).

Image G25

BID	SIZE	ASK	SIZE
1.11	65	1.12	27
1.11	56	1.12	49
1.10	48	1.12	52
1.10	36	1.12	46
1.10	15	1.13	6
1.10	12	1.13	95
1.10	6	1.13	52
1.10	4	1.13	5
1.10	2	1.13	52
1.10	45	1.13	4
1.09	44	1.14	30
1.08	44	1.15	26

Because the Green area on the BID shrank, we know that it is only a matter of seconds until the price will break down and if it will come with momentum, it could push the price even lower than our entry at $1.09. **This is a signal for us to exit the trade.** In addition to that, when I see Level 2 like this, I only focus on green and yellow price levels, I ignore the blue and pink ones.

The momentum when pushing the price up

As you noticed, a couple of times I have mentioned, that when a certain price level breaks, the price will jump and break more levels. Let me explain why. First, let's look at our Level 2 (*Image G26*).

Image G26

BID	SIZE	ASK	SIZE
1.11	112	1.12	86
1.11	2	1.13	13
1.11	16	1.13	49
1.11	28	1.13	2
1.11	15	1.13	20
1.11	12	1.13	9
1.11	6	1.13	5

We have 86 shares size on the ASK at $1.12. The Time & Sales speed is increasing, and the size is getting smaller. It changes 86>71>52>49>25>12. Our Level 2 is looking like this *(Image G27)*.

Image G27

BID	SIZE	ASK	SIZE
1.11	112	1.12	12
1.11	2	1.13	13
1.11	16	1.13	49
1.11	28	1.13	2
1.11	15	1.13	20
1.11	12	1.13	9
1.11	6	1.13	5

We have 12 shares available on the ASK at $1.12 (*Image G27*). Time and Sales and Level 2 is signalling us that the price will move up in a moment. We are about to hit our buy button for 10 shares, but we need to understand that there are thousands of other traders who are watching this stock at this given moment. All of them were waiting for the size on the ASK to get small so they could enter just before the price moved up. So we have 12 shares left on the ASK at $1.12 and many traders hitting buy button at the same time. Some of them will get some shares at $1.12, but once all orders are filled at this price level, it will automatically move to $1.13 and other traders will get filled at $1.13. And once all orders are filled at $1.13 the price will move to $1.14 and others will get filled at this price. The more participants during these moves, the stronger the moves will be.

When traders use momentum for their trading, they usually enter using Market orders or Marketable Limit Orders. Which means they will buy on the ASK no matter what the price is, or they will buy on the ASK up to a certain price level. If we look back at our example (*Image G27*), I would place a marketable limit order with $1.15 maximum entry. Which means either I will get filled from $1.12 to $1.15, or if the prices surge fast, I will not get filled at the higher price.

Another important signal on Level 2

Here is another Level 2 which signals to me that the price might go up fast (*Image G28*).

Image G28

BID	SIZE	ASK	SIZE
5.79	8	5.82	2
5.79	3	5.83	1
5.78	7	5.87	4
5.77	6	5.95	2
5.77	4	6.15	4
5.76	12	6.30	9
5.76	6	6.48	5

As you can see, there are orders on the BID at every price level. This gives me confidence because the price will not drop too fast due to the resistance at every price level. Now if we look at the ASK, we can see it is a totally different situation. There are gaps between price levels and if few price levels would get filled, the price would go up really fast. This provides low risk and high reward traders. If you enter at $5.82, you can place your stop at $5.75 - $5.76 which would be $0.07-0.08 while your target would be $6.48 and that's $0.64.

If you have the opposite Level 2 where the BID is scarce and the ASK is really thick, you should avoid trading such stock since Level 2 is signalling that the price might drop down and do it fast.

I understand it looks simple when the Level 2 is on a piece of paper and not moving. That's why I suggest spending a lot of time studying what is written so far. Level 2 is the most important tool in momentum trading and you should be an expert at it to utilise it. Trading without it is like driving with your closed eyes. Slowly you will begin recognizing situations like I showed in my examples and the better you will get at it, the more entries and exits you will notice.

CHAPTER 9
IMPORTANT INFORMATION

In this chapter I will cover many different tools and situations that you might have questions about. Again, this is my perception of these tools and circumstances, where other traders would have a different approach. Read it, understand it, and then adapt it to your own trading style.

Risk and Reward or R/R, and Stop Loss
When I started learning trading I came across this ratio - Risk/Reward. Everywhere it was written that I should seek 1:2 R/R which means for every dollar I risk, I should make 2 dollars. Every Youtube video I was watching was saying the same. To make it sound even juicier, you need to be only 50% of the time correct to be a profitable trader. And believe me, because of this ratio I almost quit learning trading. I understood its concept and how it works, but the problem that I was dealing with was the price never reaching the 2R target or reaching it way less than 50% of the time. And this made me so unmotivated because I had no idea how people reached that 2R target.

In addition to that, the second I placed the order with a stop I would feel that I made a mistake right away. Because I was looking at the large cap stocks and priced above $50. If I placed a tight stop, I would get shaken out by the market. If I placed a large stop loss - the 2R target seemed unreachable.

I spent a lot of time testing and checking to adjust my strategy. For momentum trading there is no set Risk or Reward. The main guideline I follow is this Risk/Reward ratio - 1/1. It means for every dollar I risk, I should make a dollar. But I do not pay much attention to this. Since this strategy is based on lower priced stocks at $1-8, every cent matters here and has a bigger impact than the stocks that are priced at +$50 simply because your size trading lower priced stocks will be bigger.

My stop loss varies from $0.02 to $0.10. It all depends on the price action and how choppy/volatile it is. Sometimes I will enter a trade and exit after a few seconds at the same price because of the information I see on Level 2 and Time & Sales. Some of you might say that commissions will be unbearable, but don't forget - I don't place trades on every move, I wait for momentum setup. The $0.10 is my hard stop, no matter what, if the price flushes down, I will exit at $0.10 loss a share.

Sometimes I will let the price drop to $-0.07 because I know there is a massive BID there and until it's taken out (or almost taken out), I will hold my long position.

How do I manage my risk? I explained to you how I use my stops, now let me explain how I take my profits off.

Let's say I enter the trade (Long) at a price of $1.50 with a position of 1000 shares. The price is moving up and my eyes are glued to Level 2 and Time & Sales. At $1.54 I notice a little price resistance and I will take 15% of my position off on the ASK. If the price comes back to my entry position, I will exit at the break even knowing that my initial idea is not working. If the price goes to $1.58, I will take another 15% off of my remaining position. Depending, if the price moves fast to $1.60 I will take 50% of my remaining position on the BID, if slowly - 50% on the ASK. I will give a little bit of time for the price to break $1.60. If this does not happen, I will exit the rest of my position.

Again, the increase of the price amount is not set in stone, I might take profit when the price goes up $0.03 or even wait for the price to go up $0.10 to take half of the position off. It all depends on Level 2.

There is no set in stone Risk/Reward when trading momentum.

Volume

I see Volume from 2 different angles:

1) Daily volume which helps me to see if the stock is tradeable in the pre-market and it will be good to watch it while the market is open. As I mentioned before, there is no set amount of volume, but when you look at your Gappers Scanner, look at the 5 stocks with the most traded volume for the day and start analysing them one by one to see if they fulfil the rest of our requirements.

Sometimes certain stocks will start surging up when the market is already open. Let's say at 10:30 AM certain stock starts going up, gaining momentum and at the same time its volume is increasing. Just because it has 200,000 shares traded so far, doesn't mean this stock will be untradeable. After 5 minutes this stock can have 1-2 millions shares traded.

In the pre-market it is more about the total traded volume since these stocks will have a cleaner price action. But once the market is open it's about how clean the price is and if it has the momentum. To visualise it simply - imagine that volume/second defines how clean the price action is. The higher the volume per second, the higher chances that this stock is momentum one and you will be able to read price action easier and trade it easier.

2) Volume on 1 minute and 5 minute charts

It took me a long time to understand what "trade when the volume comes in" means. When I started learning trading, I couldn't wrap my head around it. I would look at one candle and then I would look at the candle that is forming waiting for it to close to compare the volume.

Here is a simple rule to know if the volume is increasing that applies to every time frame - when you have 2 candles and the second candle is still forming, if the second candle already has as much volume as the previous one - the volume is increasing.

Let's make a little example. We have one minute candle with volume of 100,00 shares, and then we have a second 1 minute candle with 80,000 shares of volume, but still has 30 seconds until it closes. At this moment we will presume that volume is increasing and expect a price surge. We don't know how much volume the second candle will actually have, but at that given moment, we should presume that the volume is increasing.

I don't focus much on the volume during the momentum trading, but I still keep an eye on it. Daily volume doesn't matter much, especially once the market is open, so clean price action is more important which only comes with volume.

All I want to see is if the price of the stock is rising and the volume is rising accordingly. But this doesn't mean that if the price moves from $1.00 to $3.00 volume should be over the roof. When the momentum comes, the volume comes with it and keeps the pace. To make it more simple to imagine:

The road is the price, and the further you go the higher the price gets.

Momentum and volume is speed. Once it starts, it goes from 20 mph to 160 mph. Now we maintain 160 mph, the volume (and momentum) stays the same, but the price is still rising because we are getting further and further on the road. I hope this analogy makes sense.

What is more, you need to be aware of two abnormalities in the volume:

a) The price is increasing, but the volume is not. Most of the time this is a trap for people who are going Long. Usually this happens together with ASK price levels increasing, but the BID staying at the same price level. After a few moments the price flushes down and hits the stops of those people who just entered as Longs.

b) The price is staying the same, but the volume is increasing. This mostly happens when there is a massive seller on the ASK or a Hidden seller. As we saw before, Time & Sales helps us to notice these sellers. Volume could be used as a second confirmation, but I still prefer looking only at the Time & Sales so I wouldn't need to shift my focus.

There are some traders that use RVOL in addition to the volume. I don't use this indicator because if the stock has a high RVOL it doesn't mean that it is tradeable and fits our parameters. The same goes for volume. Even if the stock has a massive volume, the price action could be really dirty. I don't see the point of using a second indicator which provides the same outcome.

Volatility
Volatility often refers to the amount of uncertainty or risk related to the size of changes in a security's value. A higher volatility means that a security's value can potentially be spread out over a larger range of values (Investopedia).

Now, every trader understands volatility differently. For me, volatility is price movement when the price tends to fluctuate in a wider range. It is a part of momentum trading. If there is no volatility, there is no opportunity in day trading.

Here how clean price action with a little bit of volatility looks like (*Image H1*).

Image H1

And here is an example of not clean and volatile price action (*Image H2*).

Image H2

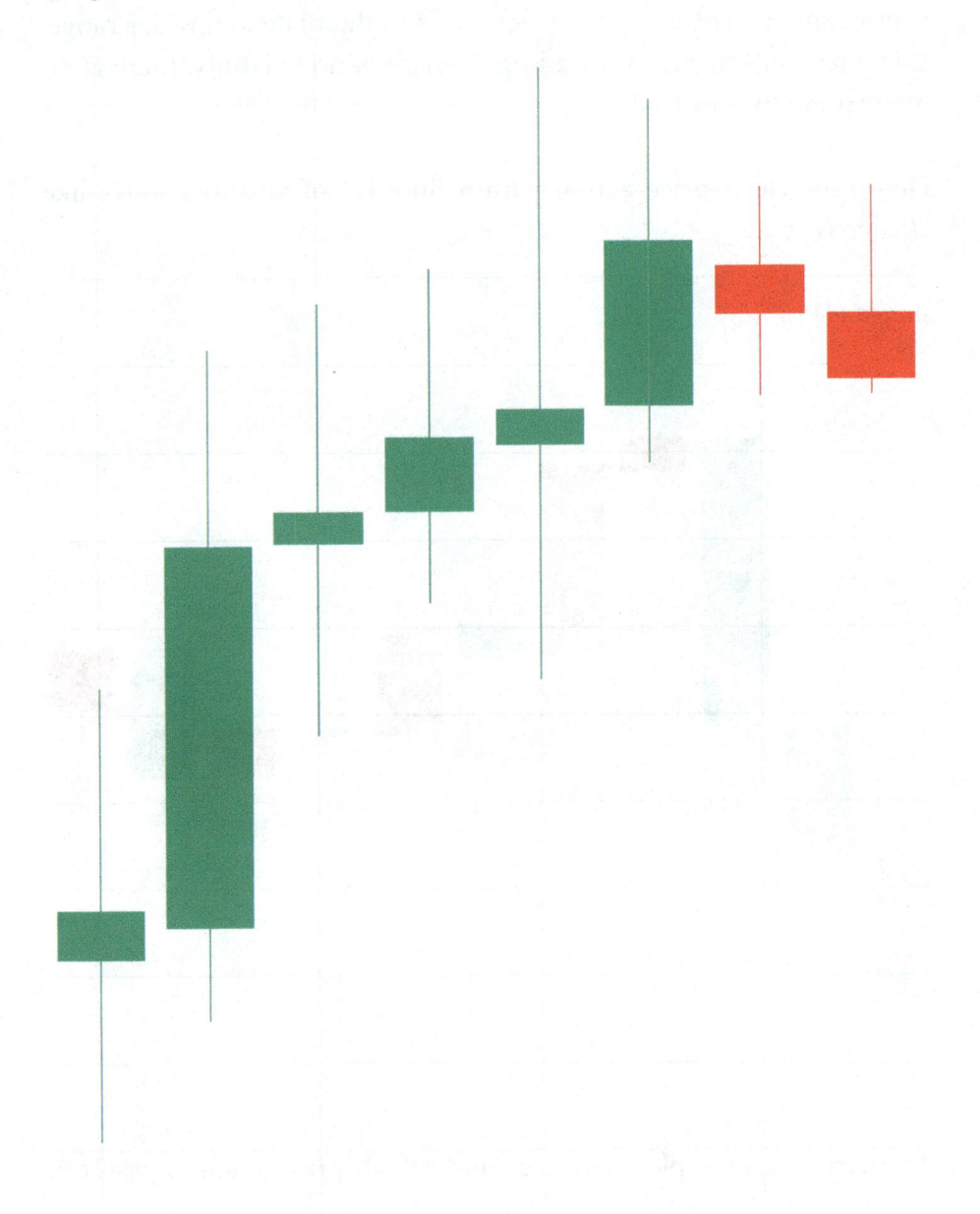

After comparing these two images, we can define volatility as the increased amount and length of the candle wicks. And whenever you notice such candles, try to stay away from trading such stocks. The worst scenario is when the stock is trading nice and has a clean price action, but slowly transforms into a volatile one and you get sucked into it. Later on I will provide an example of how to avoid getting sucked into it.

Indicators

As every beginning trader, I had a full screen of indicators where I could barely see the main price chart. Elliot Waves, Bollinger Band, RSI, MACD, Camarillo levels and many more. I even spent hours trying to understand how they are calculated. However, I ended up using none of them.

Like I mentioned before, I try to shave off time wherever I can and the time that I would spend looking at the indicators I wouldn't spend on Level 2.

Here is the list of every indicator that I use:

Daily chart:
- Simple Moving Average 9
- Simple Moving Average 20
- Simple Moving Average 50
- Simple Moving Average 100
- Simple Moving Average 200

The best case is when the price is above all moving averages, but I would still trade the stock when the price is under two or three moving averages 200 SMA, 100 SMA and 50 SMA. If it's under 20 SMA and below, I would trade that stock.

DAY TRADING

Here is a perfect example when the price is trading above all moving averages (*Image H3*).

Image H3

[chart image]

5 minute chart:
- 9 Exponential Moving Average
- 20 Exponential Moving Average
- Volume Weighted Average price

The price has to be always trading above VWAP no matter what. As for 9 EMA and 20 EMA, I would still be looking for an entry when the prices come back to these Averages, but I would be more cautious due to the fact that the stock might have lost the momentum.

Image H4

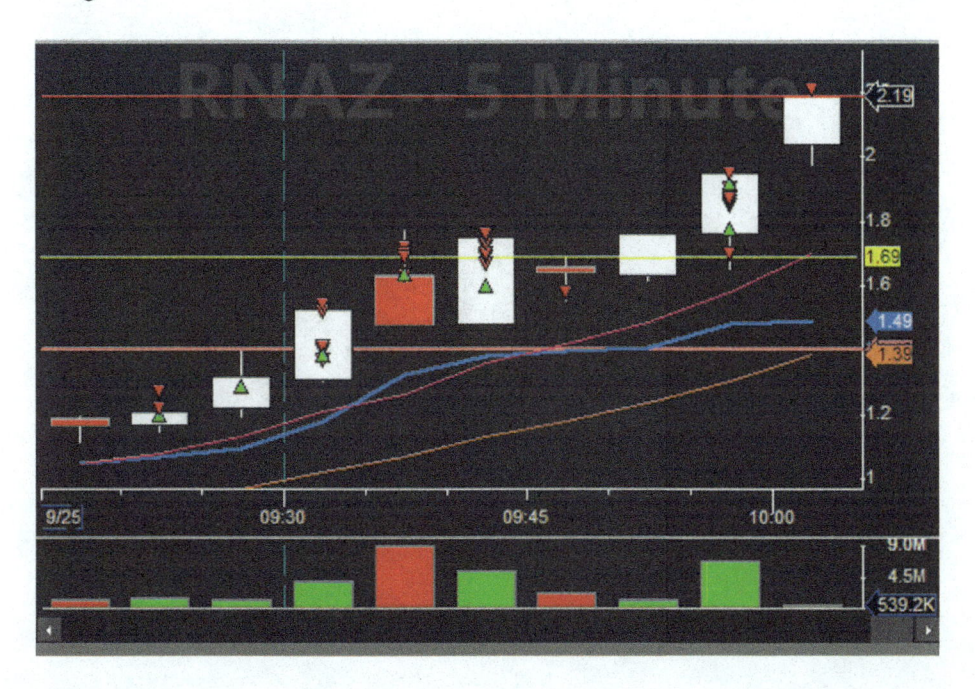

As you can see in the picture above *(Image H4)*, the price since the market opened, has been trading above Blue (VWAP), Pink (9 EMA) and Orange (20 EMA) lines

1 minute chart:
- 9 Exponential Moving Average
- 20 Exponential Moving Average
- Volume Weighted Average price

Image H5

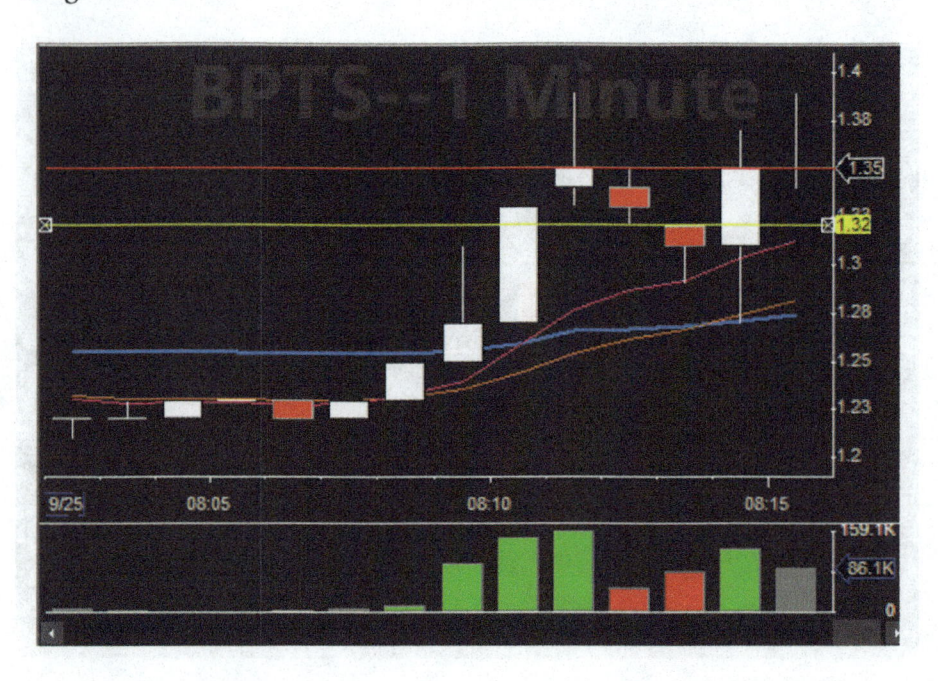

[chart image]

Same as on the 5 minute chart - the price always has to be above VWAP on 1 minute chart as well. If it is below it, it's a massive sign of weakness and I wouldn't touch it. As for moving averages, when the price surges up and then pulls back to 9 EMA or 20 EMA, it offers one of the best entry levels since you can place your stop at the moving average, however, there is less momentum during that period.

Answer to many, yes, I do know that moving averages are lagging indicators and show what has already happened, but so many people use it that they actually provide resistance and support. It does not mean that the price will go to the exact price level of the moving average, but you should use this knowledge and capitalise on it.

Size of the position
This is a really tricky question and there are many different answers to it. Some say it's a certain percentage of your capital, or the max loss

limit should be a certain percentage of your buying power, or even how much risk you can handle. And all of these answers are correct.

For me, personally, placing trades using this formula made my life easier:

"$5000/Share price"

I am not sure if your trading platform provides such a function, but it saves me a lot of time. You could do it manually with a calculator or even in your head if you can.

Handling risk means how much you get affected mentally when the price drops per 1 cent.

Let's say the price of the stock is $2.00. I press my buy button and using this "$5000/share price" function a trade gets placed and filled. Now I have 2500 shares. If the price goes down by 1 cent, I have unrealized profit at 2500 x -0.01$ = -$25. One tick and that's $25 dollars down. Price gets a little choppy and it drops to $1.94. I am down to -$150 and then remember to add commissions. If you think you couldn't handle such price movement, lower the amount of dollars to "$3000/share price" or even "$1000/share price". It all depends on how comfortable you are, or how much risk you can handle. I suggest starting small and slowly increasing the dollar size.

With what I just said, you need to take into account the price of the stock. Because using this formula "$/share price" you purchase a lesser amount of higher priced stocks which leads to smaller risk that needs to be handled.

Image H6

Size	Price	Amount	1c move
$5000	$10	500	$5
$5000	$1	5000	$50
$5000	$0.70	7143	$71.43

As per table above, the risk changes depending on the price of stock. To make more manageable I have 3 different buttons to place orders with following functions:

Image H7

Function	Share price	1c move
$7000/share price	$5 and above	$14 or less
$5000/share price	$1 - $5	$10 - $50
$2500/share price	$0.70 - $1	$25 - $35

I don't need to do any calculations during my trading. I see how much the stock costs and hit the buy button that fits this table's price bracket.

I highly suggest using this system, of course, if your trading platform supports it. And do not forget to adjust the size of the dollars to your comfort.

I would like to add one more important rule that I follow during my trading. Usually I start trading at 8:30 AM. It doesn't mean I place the orders right away, but I start looking for tradable stocks. For me 8:30 AM - 9:30 AM is the pre-market. And most of the times the size of the positions will be half or even a quarter of the original position. So instead of "$5000/share price", it will be "$1500-2500/share price". And there are 3 reasons for that. The premarket movement is not clean as during trading hours and by reducing the position I reduce my risk and exposure. There are no "Trading Halts" during premarket which means the price of the stock can skyrocket or plummet. And lastly, I use these trades as warm up. If I make little gains I gain a little confidence, If I have little losses - it's all right, it was the price of the warm up and it will not affect my ability to trade when the market opens. However, there are days when certain stocks move so clean and fast in the premarket that I place full orders as if the market would be already open.

How deep you need to look into Level 2
This depends on how much information you can perceive any given moment. It's really up to everyone's preference and trading style. Understand how I use it and try to adapt to your own style. Here is an example of my Level 2 on lower priced stock (*Image H8*).

Image H8

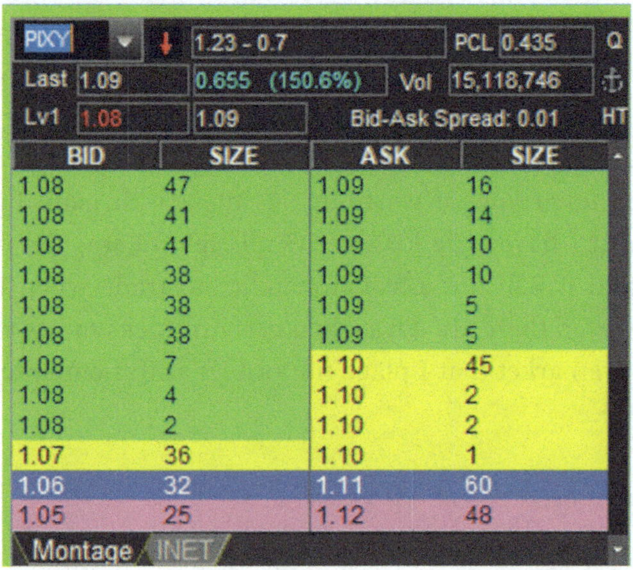

And this is how it looks on higher priced stock (*Image H9*).

Image H9

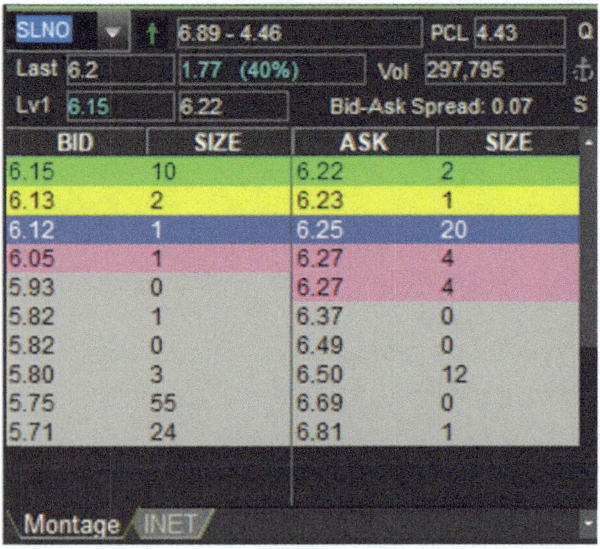

I never change the size of my Level 2. The stock price doesn't matter, the price levels don't matter - always the same size because my eyes know where to look right away. The most confusion for traders comes from the amount of price levels seen on Level 2. I see 10 price levels and 4 of them are colour coded which are most important to me.

In the first example of the "PIXY" ticker, you can see the price range on the BID from $1.05 to $1.08 while on the "SLNO" ticker - from $5.71 to $6.15 on the BID.

The lower the price of the stock, the more concentrated orders on Level 2 will be. And this is because 1 cent move is more impactful on $1 priced stock than $10 priced stock. In addition to that, it shows how thick or thin Level 2 is and how many people are participating at the moment.

You can have high priced stock and have thick Level 2. Here is an example (*Image H10*).

Image H10

BID	SIZE	ASK	SIZE
20.54	151	20.55	455
20.54	117	20.55	455
20.54	100	20.55	439
20.54	96	20.55	316
20.54	91	20.55	242
20.54	91	20.55	212
20.54	56	20.55	117
20.54	11	20.55	114
20.54	1	20.55	111
20.53	269	20.55	85
20.53	127	20.55	76
20.53	108	20.55	56

What is more, you probably noticed that I don't have MMID (Market Maker's ID) on my Level 2. It does provide a little bit of information, but because the price movement is so fast on Momentum stocks, I solely focus on price and size. The amount of time that it would require me to keep looking at MMID is way too much. This is another place where I shave the time off.

There is another important piece of information that we need to talk about - large orders on Level 2 that are further away from the current price. To make it more simple to explain, we will use my homemade Level 2 again, but with deeper Level 2 *(Image H11)*.

Image H11

BID	SIZE	ASK	SIZE
$5.49	2	$5.50	3
$5.47	5	$5.52	4
$5.40	4	$5.55	2
$5.37	3	$5.56	3
$5.36	3	$5.59	5
$5.31	8	$5.61	7
$5.29	3	$5.69	5
$5.27	2	$5.75	4
$5.26	2	$5.85	5
$5.02	236	$5.97	485
$5.01	1	$5.99	2

Sometimes we see these massive orders appearing on Level 2. Most of the time I don't see them because my Level 2 is pretty small and

I trade only momentum stocks which have pretty thick Level 2. But either way, let's talk about how to perceive this information.

Some of the traders see it as an opportunity. If they see a massive order on ASK which is pretty far away from current price, they will take it as a bullish signal because the price will come to that order. And the opposite is if they see a massive BID which is further away from the current price.

I, personally, ignore these far away from the current price orders on Level 2. First, I don't see them most of the time because my Level 2 window is pretty small and second they are too far from the current price. By the time the price goes up or down to that price level, these orders can be removed by the traders who placed it. But if they stay when the price is getting closer to them, I will start paying more and more attention to them. Simply put - if they are close they are important, if they are far away - they are not important.

News and Catalysts
For momentum trading I do not use any information that comes from news sources. Sometimes I will put TV News on just for the background noise. My trading news comes from my trading scanners. They tell me what stocks are breaking the high of the day or surging on high volume. There might be news on these stocks, but all it matters to me is the price action which has to be clean.

However, there is one tool that I use - Voice news. Most of the time it's just background noise for me, but once I hear "Ticker "x" made a new high" or "Ticker "y" got halted to the upside", I will pay attention to it and check these stocks on my charts and Level 2. But having scanners is enough because Voice news provides the same information as scanners, but it helps to save some time instead of looking at the scanner.

There are many reasons why stocks move and we can never know why. If the stock does not have a catalyst, but has huge volume and clean price action - I will trade it. It's impossible to know why prices are moving. Some people might say that if you take 2 stocks that trade identically, the one with the catalyst will be better than the one without it. I will never understand such a statement because it is incorrect. There are so many catalysts on many stocks every day, but all of them do not provide clean price action. Only price action shows that stock has a clean price action.

Another important topic - SPY (SPDR S&P 500 ETF Trust). This ticker is watched by hundreds of millions of people. And to many of these people it provides a lot of information for their trading strategies.

The reason why I never trade such stocks as MSFT, AAPL, or NVDA, is that they are heavily impacted by the SPY. Most of their price movement is identical to the SPY price movement. On certain days, when these stocks have impactful news, they will deviate from SPY and trade independently. After 2-3 days these stocks will be doing exactly the same thing again as SPY is doing. Why not to trade these stocks when they have news or catalyst? Because most of these stocks who follow SPY are large cap stocks and their price movement is different from low cap stocks. The difference is colossal. I find these stocks untradeable, especially on a smaller time frame. Don't get me wrong, there are many profitable traders who trade them and trade them well.

I used to have one chart dedicated just for watching SPY. You know, take a glance at it from time to time in case the market is crashing. But after some time I realised that I would look at the SPY chart before putting my trade on a low priced stock, and if the SPY would have a large red bar to the downside, I would not place the trade. The price of that low priced stock would surge up, but without me. After some time I realised that if there will be a market crash, I will find out about it from my scanners or Voice news. I don't use SPY charts anymore.

Algorithmic trading
Many of you heard about "algos" and their existence. They do take up most of the daily trading volume on the market, but their impact on momentum trading is almost non-existent.

We are trading stocks that are surging up on massive volume, breaking various resistance levels. Sometimes the price gets so far from moving averages that it takes hours for it to come back. For "algos" such price movement is irrational. In addition to that, there are so many participants, real traders, which makes it impossible for "algos" to predict the price movement. Of course, I do not say that there are no "algos" at all that trade such price movements, but their impact is so little that we do not need to worry about them.

On the same note, I would like to mention "dark pools" and "Over-The-Counter" trading. We do know that these trading methods exist, but it does not affect our trading system. It is basically impossible for retail traders to access such information, and its impact is so small to momentum stocks, that we do not even think about them.

Spread
As most of you know, the spread is the price between BID and ASK. And the best it would be if you could see it as easily as possible.

Image H12

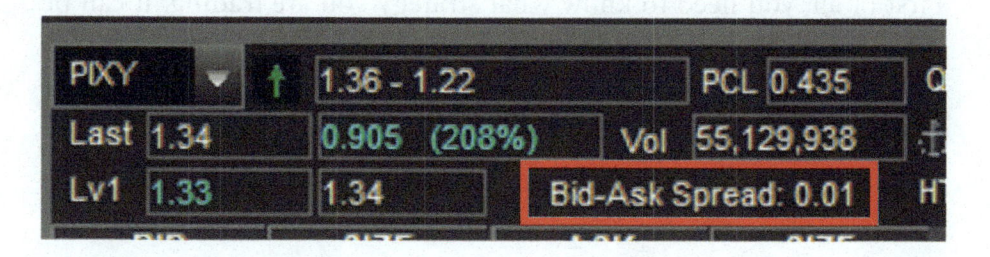

My Bid-Ask spread is integrated into the Level 2 top panel, next to the Level 1. Once I choose the stock and press enter, my first millisecond is checking the spread.

The best possible spread is $0.01 for any stock trading at $1.00 and above.

The maximum bearable spread for me personally is $0.05. And even at this spread price I am not very comfortable.

Another important thing to note, the larger the spread, the thinner Level 2 is. Which means there will be bigger price gaps between price levels and it is one of our parameters that have to be validated to even consider trading such stock. These stocks can still provide great opportunities and you can profit from them, but you need to have a different approach to them.

What does it mean "waiting for the price to come"?
If you know the meaning of it, you can skip this part, but because it took me so long to understand the nuance of it, I will explain to those who don't know.

When I started learning trading I learnt about patterns, I could see them forming, but couldn't process the waiting for the price.

First of all, you need to know what strategy you are trading. It can be Break of the High of Day, or ABCD or Cup and Handle. Every strategy has its own entry points at certain price levels. We are going to use the ABCD strategy for our example (*Image H13*).

Image H13

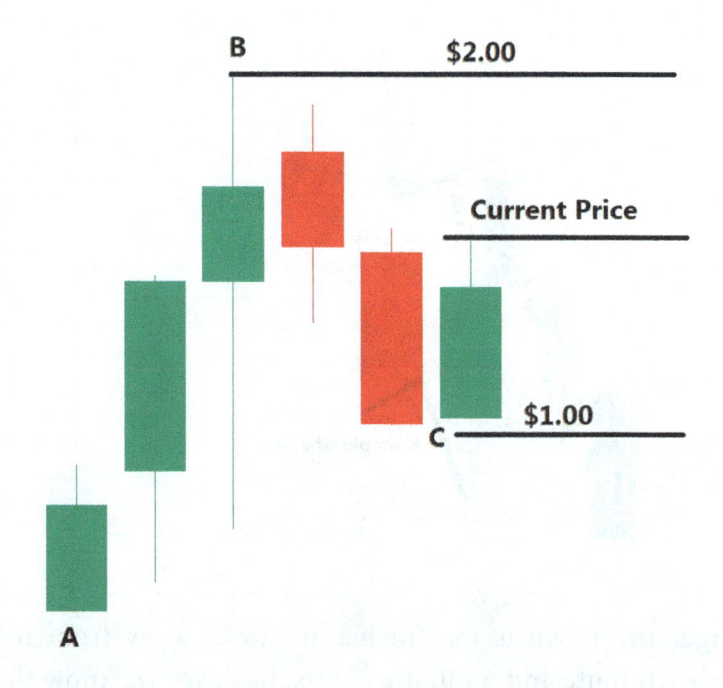

Because we are trading ABCD strategy, our entry area is at B which is $2.00. We can see that the current price is trading between $1.00 and $2.00. As long as the price is trading above $1.00 the C level, the pattern and strategy are still valid. Now you are only waiting for the price to come to the B level where you would enter the trade. This is "waiting for the price to come".

Extended prices
We see and assume that the price is extended when it surges up without pullbacks. There are many variations of it, but the easiest way to describe it would be - when the price moves so fast up, it doesn't offer any pullback entries on the 5 minute chart except the break of the previous candle's high.

Image H14

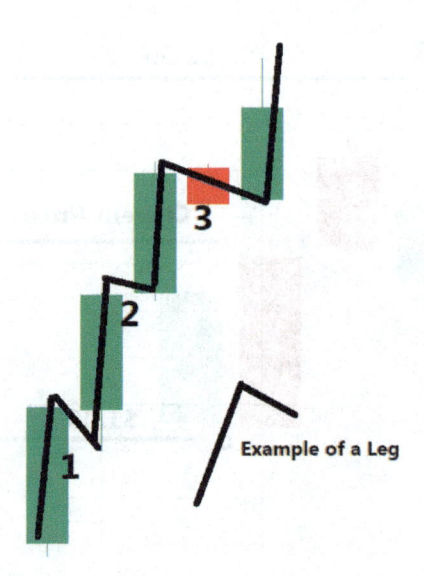

Example of a Leg

The stronger the move is the further it moves away from moving averages on 1 minute and 5 minute charts, however we know that the price, at some point, tends to pull back to the moving averages. The further up the price moves the riskier it gets because there are less and less participants. Of course, there are days when the price will just go up without looking back leaving those moving averages way behind, but that does not happen often. The safest rule that most traders follow is trading only the first two Legs. After that you can still look for entries, but you need to understand that you will be taking more risk and the chances of having a false breakout are increasing. I do trade 3rd and 4th legs, but the Level 2 has to be sending strong signals for strong support and aggressive buyers.

No matter how strong the stock is, it will always pull back, no matter what and no one knows when. Just to know, if the price surges up and then pulls back into a consolidation, on the 5 minute chart it will be a first leg. Because the price got into consolidation, the number of legs on the 1 minute chart are reset. It means when the price makes a new high and forms a new leg on a 1 minute chart, it will be the first leg again.

Important price levels
As we learnt already, we get our price levels from the charts. Now, there are many price levels, but we need to choose the most important ones. If you have too many of them, it might look that the stock will never go up because of the amount of the resistance lines you have.

Here is my list:
- High of the previous days. Nothing else matters, if the stock is not trading above previous day high, I will not be touching it;
- Moving Averages on 1 minute, 5 minute and Daily charts;
- Pre-Market high. Very important level, especially when the market opens. Breaking and trading above pre-market levels signals a strong signal;
- The high of the day. Probably the most important one;
- The high of the move, or top pivot point;
- The low of the move, or bottom pivot point.

Crucial to know, that when the price surges up and breaks a resistance line, that resistance line becomes the support line and the price should hold it, which means it shouldn't go below it. In addition to that, I never have more than three price level lines on my chart.

Other price levels that I always keep an eye on are full dollar prices and half dollar prices. I never draw lines through them, but many traders use these levels as support or resistance.

The best times to trade
As you know, I usually sit down at the computer and start looking for possible stocks to trade, usually at 8:30 AM. The best time I find to

start is 8:30 AM - 9:00 AM because you can catch a couple easy trades since the market is pretty calm.

If I start too late, after 9:00 AM, I will not place any trades until the market opens. I get this feeling that I missed action and I need to put some trades on to catch up.

No matter what, I will not be placing any trades from 9:20 AM to 9:30 AM.

Most of the time I will not place any trade from 9:30 AM to 9:35 AM because the price action gets too hectic and volatile. The only possible play would be a break of the high of the day, micro pullback, and then I would enter on the move up. However, trading the first 5 minutes is too risky and the risk is not worth the reward.

I will usually end my trading day at 11:00 AM unless there is a stock that has a great price action and offers good opportunities. I find that if I stay any longer than that, I become more reckless. Another important reason is that from 9:30 AM to 11:00 AM all my focus is on the trading and believe it or not, it gets really exhausting. It's not just physical exhaustion, but mental as well.

These are my trading times, but you need to work on yourself and find which time works the best for you. Just to know, after 12:00 AM, the market really cools down and the amount of stocks that move on great volume with clean price actions is only a handful.

Some traders use high of the day/move as a target price
Yes, this is a valid price level and we should use it, even when trading momentum. When I started trading it took me a while to understand how and when the high of the day or high of the move is the target.

Image H15

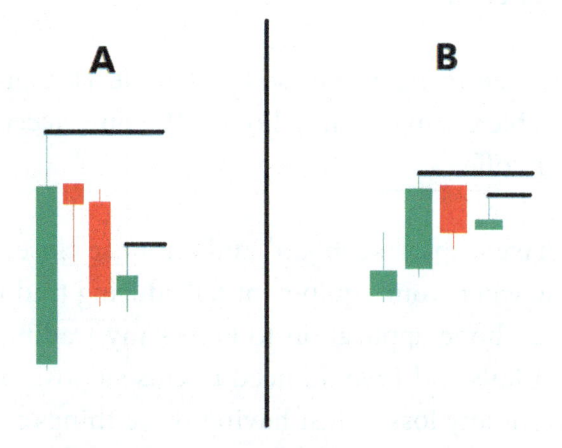

As in the picture (*Image H15*), you can see that A chart has a large range from the current price and the high of the day or the high of the move. If you would enter now, we could use this as our target. While in the B chart this range is so small and if you are planning to put a trade on, you need to be expecting that the price will break the high of the day/move, otherwise the risk would not be worth the reward.

To put it simply, if the pullback is strong, around 50% of the initial move, then I would consider the high of that move as a target. Many strategies, especially the ones that have entry when the price pulls back to the moving averages, have high of the day/move as their target.

Mental preparation
There is much literature about trading psychology so I will tell you only what works and helps me.

As I mentioned before, not being in the rush is really important to me. This means sitting at my computer at a certain time. In addition to that, I don't have any other tasks until 11:00 AM. No meetings, no grocery shopping, no doctor appointments. If it happens that I have to attend one of the mentioned events during my trading hours - I will not trade that day at all, not even in the premarket.

Having breakfast before the trading so I will not feel hungry or peckish. No food at the table during trading hours. The only acceptable option is a cup of tea or coffee.

Making sure I have a spare keyboard and a mouse close to me. There is nothing worse when your equipment fails during trading. Recently, I started using a phone application to access my trading platform in case the internet fails and I would need to close a position as soon as possible to prevent any losses. Just having these things ready puts me at ease.

I have my headphones on while I am trading. From 8:30 AM to 9:20 AM I will have CNBC playing in the background. It does not provide any information that would help for my trading, but it helps to keep my mind active while I listen to it passively. What is more, premarket can be very slow sometimes so it helps me not to get bored.

I do use trading chat, but I am very strict about it. I never post when I enter a trade or when I exit the trade. I never post how much I made or lost that day. All I do is share my thoughts on possible trades like: "FEMY is moving", "PLTR is holding its 9 EMA in 1 minute", "UTCI got halted" and similar things. And since most of the people in these chats trade only the most active stocks, this information helps them in case they missed it. The same works for me, I always keep an eye on the chat in case the scanner has missed a great move or I just didn't notice it. I personally found that this free chat on Youtube is the best for me because there are not too many people spamming in the chat, and since it's not paid, there is no agenda from the administration. You can find the chat here: https://www.Youtube.com/@STOCKSROCKS (the chat is active only when the channel is live).

They have been streaming every day for years now and provide scanners plus voice news with 2 minute delays. I'm using my own scanners without the delay, but the chat is still an important source for trading. I pop the chat out and move it next to my platform on my main trading screen so I can always see if someone posted information about that stock that I might have missed.

It's up to every trader to decide what works for them and what to do to maintain focus during trading. I highly suggest reading a couple of books about trading psychology, use what you find useful and adapt to your routine. Whenever you find yourself doing what you shouldn't or a distraction, make sure you eliminate it for future success.

Importance of breakeven
I want to emphasise how important it is to exit your trade if it's not working out. Becoming good at it can turn you into a profitable trader without any major changes to your strategy.

Momentum trading requires resolution in less than a minute, most of the time even less. If Level 2 is signalling that the price can't break a certain level or you notice that there is a hidden seller - exit your position. In the long run you will save a lot of money.

It is really hard to change to this concept if you have been trading for years and especially on the larger time frames. This idea of exiting at breakeven or at little loss is not so popular in the trading literature where you have to stick to your stops.

You need to understand that I do not spam trades until I get lucky. I enter only when I see signals on Level 2. If the price can't break a certain level I will exit the trade at breakeven or at a little loss. I am not going to enter again when the price comes back to that level, I will wait until it breaks it.

Hotkeys

If you are not using hotkeys you should not try trading momentum. The time you would waste on setting up the entry or exit would take too much time and it could be fatal to your account. Here are my main hotkeys:

- Buy - a marketable limit order with $0.05 offset with a funcion "$/share price". Which means I am giving a little room for the slippage;
- Sell ALL - a market order to sell on the BID;
- Sell 50% of the remaining position on the BID;
- Sell 15% of the remaining position on the ASK;
- Breakeven order;

It took me a lot of time to get used to selling into the ASK, but once I mastered it, it really changed my performance and profitability. I use "Sell 15% of the remaining position on the ASK" to reduce my position and lock in some profits when the price is surging up. Because I am selling into the ASK, I am making extra $0.01 - $0.02 on every sold share.

The other hotkeys are generic and I've adjusted them to my trading style. What is more, I never turn a green trade into a red trade, no matter what.

Scanners

I use two types of scanners: Gappers list and Momo HOD scanner.

The gappers list scanner I use mostly when I start my trading day. I will look for the stocks that are suitable for momentum trading. After that, I will not pay anymore attention to the gappers list.

Image H16

Gappers: 10:30:45 - 10:31:14 6/20/2023

Symbol	Price ($)	Gap (%)	Flt (Shr)	Shrt Flt (%)	Vol Today	Vol 5 Min	Earn Date
EFOI	2.04	610.1	10.5M	1.48	35,907	160.0	39.25
GSRMR	2.55	60.0			103,393	2,477	
DICE	46.50	37.5	38.4M	26.23	11.55M	10,677	37.75
VCIG	4.07	35.0	2.15M	0.69	31.14M	5,528	
BOF	5.42	31.6			6.35M	893.4	
NUWE	3.23	26.6	1.20M	1.98	8.31M	9,220	35.25
LUCY	2.23	21.5	3.50M	1.83	10.02M	4,633	
ZURAW	0.5399	19.5	14.4M		9,700	0.0	
CANO	1.48	17.6	222M	10.71	4.94M	197.4	36.75
GRFX	1.32	16.0	20.3M		28,678	0.0	
CING	0.9897	15.7	8.05M	2.32	42,292	0.0	
CNTG	0.8200	15.3	14.3M	0.37	21,048	0.0	-0.75
QUOT	3.90	15.2	88.5M	1.80	2.28M	816.3	35.75
SEED	4.39	14.9	4.76M	0.21	13,788	105.3	20.25
VERA	15.34	13.4	26.6M	8.53	799,506	458.3	37.25
BLDEW	0.6474	13.4			7,003	0.0	
LUNRW	0.6360	12.9	6.04M		12,101	0.0	
VALN	16.89	12.6	46.6M		24,510	1,270	
CJET	2.84	12.3	14.3M		157,753	2.9	
ICAD	1.59	12.0	23.9M	1.17	5.54M	28,188	37.75
LILM	1.35	11.8	145M	4.24	3.49M	223.1	-18.75
EM	0.9000	10.5	214M		115,548	0.0	0.25
PCSA	0.5450	9.6	19.8M	0.99	25,566	0.0	37.50
AGIL	0.7798	9.6	30.2M	1.36	9,138	0.0	36.25
FNGR	2.30	9.4	21.3M	0.75	821,792	443.5	-14.25

The Momo HOD scanner shows the stock when it is making a High of the day on a relatively high volume. I use this scanner to find stocks that have momentum. In addition to that, it is set to show only low float stocks, but it's up to you how you adjust the settings *(Image H17*).

Image H17

Symbol	Time	Price ($)	Flt (Shr)	Rel Vol	Vol 1 Min	Vol Today	Shrt Flt (%)
ICAD	9:41	1.38	23.9M	80.91	4,677	458.0K	1.17
DICE	9:41	46.58	38.4M	825.76	13,520	5.75M	26.23
VCIG	9:41	4.15	2.15M	297.55	19,694	11.91M	0.69
LUCY	9:40	2.71	3.50M	65.14	96,288	7.20M	1.83
VCIG	9:39	4.14	2.15M	320.58	40,250	10.66M	0.69
VCIG	9:29	4.14	2.15M	320.58	40,250	10.66M	0.69
STRR	9:38	1.56	11.3M	96.94	8,695	235.3K	1.76
STRR	9:38	1.55	11.3M	95.99	7,906	232.5K	1.76
VCIG	9:38	3.95	2.15M	320.98	28,631	9.48M	0.69
GREE	9:37	3.29	3.09M	37.13	494.2	171.1K	7.35
GNUS	9:36	3.25	29.6M	35.38	3,956	289.9K	9.21

Most of the traders use Trade Ideas scanners, but it's a matter of a choice. If you are just learning to trade and do not want to spend money on the scanners, I suggest using https://www.Youtube.com/@STOCKSROCKS Youtube channel which provides the same scanners with 2 minutes delay. Even with that delay you will not miss many entries.

CHAPTER 10
TRADING STOCK HALTS

One of the most beautiful things that I see when trading is when the stock gets halted. There is so much misinformation about it that most people think that when the stock gets halted it is a negative thing, but they are wrong, at least from my perspective.

Stock gets halted when it surges up or surges down. I will not go into specifics, you can read somewhere else more about stock halts.

First, we try to avoid getting stuck in a halt when the price is going down. Sometimes there is nothing you can do about it and that is the price you have to pay. It might go down so fast that your Stop Loss might not work. If you are not experienced enough, I highly suggest not to trade halts.

Second, the halts that are surging up provide one of the best trading opportunities. Let's start with the most important rule - only trade first and second halts, never more. No matter how tempting it looks, stay away from the third and more halts. But you need to understand that if the stock consolidates after the halt, moves back to the moving averages, when the next halt up happens, it counts as a first halt again.

Here is an example of a halt looks on my trading platform (*Image I1*).

Image I1

BID	SIZE	ASK	SIZE
1.75	354	1.75	
1.75	324	1.76	84
1.75	324	1.76	26
1.75	168	1.76	18
1.75	137	1.76	15
1.75	125	1.76	12
1.75	81	1.76	11
1.75	43	1.76	7
1.75	19	1.76	7
1.75	10	1.76	4
1.75	9	1.76	4
1.75	3	1.76	3

RNAZ 1.78 - 1.3 PCL 0.664
Last 1.75 1.086 (163.6%) Vol 31,384,541
Lv1 1.75 1.76 Bid-Ask Spread: 0.01

Or as many traders would say - "The ASK is pinned to the top". If the price action stays like this for a certain amount of time, usually a few seconds, the price will go into the halt and will be untradeable for 5 minutes, 10 minutes or 20 minutes, depending on how many orders have to be sorted out. I never count manually how much the price has to change to get into a halt. Once I see these grey price levels showing up on my Level 2, I know that the stock soon might go into a halt.

It doesn't mean that the price will go into the halt when the ASK gets pinned to the top. The price might drop and the halt level would increase. Because the halt is calculated by how much the price changed per certain period of time and since more time passes the next level for the halt would be higher.

Before we move forward, we need to clear one stigma that is floating in many trading videos and books. Many of you heard when the stock gets halted for weeks, months, or it doesn't even ever trade again. There are many reasons why this can happen, but basically it's the Stock Exchange saying that this stock is not fulfilling its requirements to be traded on this stock exchange.

Luckily, we do not trade such stocks. The reason is simple - we trade really liquid stocks which have a smaller chance to get into such a halt. Another reason is that we have Voice news in our background which would let us know that the SEC or Stock Exchange are going to investigate certain stocks. I understand it sounds really bad that your money could get frozen for days, weeks or even months, but this mostly happens to stocks that are not that liquid. During my trading years I never worried about it and never encountered it. If you want to be on a really safe side, you should keep track of SEC or Stock Exchange notifications about investigations.

To trade Halts you have to be able to place orders and exit positions in a matter of milliseconds. If your internet connection is slow, or your platform makes you click the confirmation button - never trade halts.

There are three ways I trade halts. Remember, I trade only when the price is going up:

1) I have a position, price surges up and goes into a halt. That's the best option and it provides the least risk while the reward is the highest. Once the stock resumes trading after the halt, and the price rises, I will close 50% of the position to lock in profits. After that my eyes will be glued to Level 2 and Time & Sales. If there is another important level like 200 Moving Average just above the trading price, I will close the rest of my position;

2) The stock gets halted due to price surging up. After the halt ends, the price opens higher. I can see the price jumping up and down, but without any clear indications. The first minute closes, but the direction of the price is still unknown because of buyers and sellers fighting. Then time is going by and we have second candle forming and the 1 minute chart looks like this:

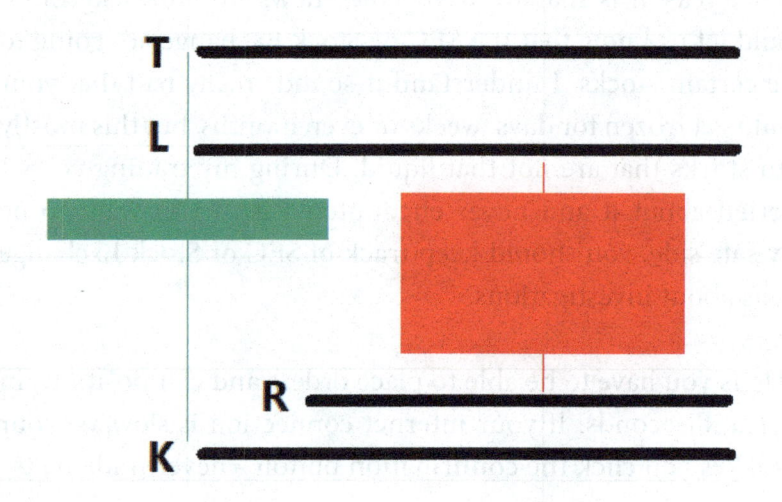

Image 12

K - The price level where the stock started trading after the halt and the low price of the first candle. It's best to avoid having a position whenever the price breaks this level because, most likely, the next thing that will happen is a halt going to the downside.

R - The low of the second candle. Even if the candle is still forming, this low provides us a certain degree of support.

The price area between K and R, is our danger area and it's a signal to close your position if you have one. It's like a little grace period which lasts a moment of the second for you to exit your trade. Once R support level is broken, most likely K will be pushed through as well, and with the momentum the price will surge down into a halt to the downside. There might be a massive support at K to hold the price, but the closer the price gets to K, the more risk there is.

L - The high of the current candle that is still forming.

T - The high of the previous candle or the first candle that formed once the stock resumed trading after the halt.

The price area between T and L, is our entry area where we should be looking for entering a position.

Such a setup, where you are looking for an entry when the price breaks the high of the candle which is still forming, is called micro pullback. I use it not only for trading halts, but when the price breaks the high of the day or even when it is squeezing up. Because during the squeeze there are no price consolidations for a few minutes to look for an entry when the candles are making higher highs.

There are many times when the price breaks out and surges up and then has a little micro pullback at the top as I mentioned before. If I see that the price is holding R price level and the stock still has momentum, I will enter a position based on the strength of the support. Here is an example of it (*Image 13*).

DAY TRADING

Image I2

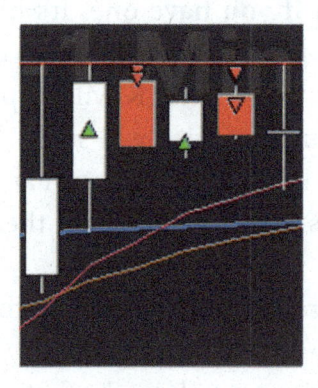

The green UP arrows are my entries and the RED down arrows are my exits. These trades were based on the strength of the support at those price levels. Some people might say that these moves were too small to make some money. My stop levels were at those price support levels, which means they were $0.01-0.02 below my entry price and I gained $0.05-0.06 per share.

Now to be more clear, this was what I saw on Level 2 and it was signalling me to exit my trades.

Image I4

Times & Sales were printing orders at $0.7 at a huge speed, however the price was not moving and once I noticed it, I started exiting my position. I will go through this trade later step by step to show you my thought process.

3) The stock gets halted due to price surging up. After the halt ends, the price opens higher. I can see the price jumping up and down, but without any clear indications. The first minute closes, but the direction of the price is still unknown because of buyers and sellers fighting. The chart looks exactly the same as before (*Image I4*).

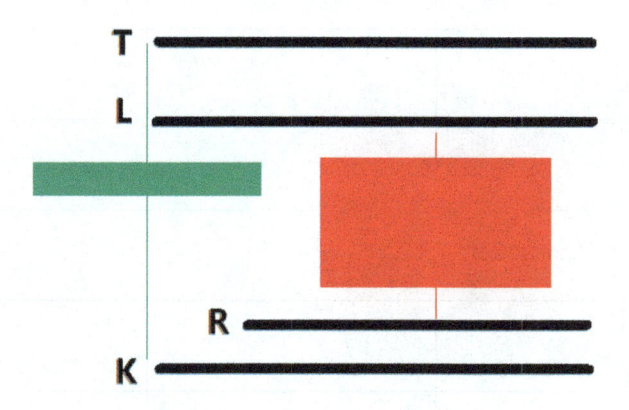

Image I5

Everything is the same, the same price levels, the same candles as in (*Image I2*). But if I see on Level 2 that the buyers are getting exhausted (Time & Sales slow down) and more time passes, I expect a fake breakout. The market would push the price to the area between T and L, people would enter their long positions, and then the market would flush the price down hitting their stops. To avoid that I would enter a position only when the price would be breaking T level and level L would be my stop area.

Keep in mind, I trade halts only that open higher than the halt level.

This type of trading halts requires a lot of focus and patience. If you misread signals or, even if the market decides not to follow the setup, be always ready to hit the exit button. I do not recommend trading halts for beginners, but what I suggest is to have a Simulation account always ready and when you see prices getting halted, switch to Simulation and trade there to gain more practice. And remember, charts provide price levels and Level 2 provides entry and exit signals.

CHAPTER 11
DEALING WITH FALSE BREAKOUTS

False breakouts are the worst enemies to every day trader. It is probably #1 reason why many traders got their accounts wiped. I was surprised how little attention is given to these false breakouts in the trading literature. There is no methodology to avoid false breakouts at 100%. The best we can do is not be participants of the market when it happens. Don't get me wrong, many traders every day get caught in false breakouts.

Let's put an example of the fake breakout in front of our eyes first (*Image J1*).

Image J1

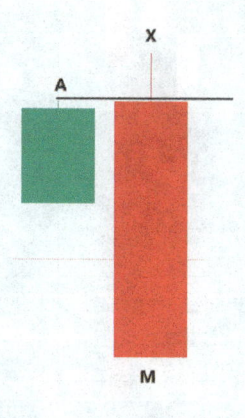

A - The highest point of the Green Candle
X - The highest point of the Red Candle
M - The lowest point of the Red Candle

We see such a pattern every single day and we all know that when the second candle makes a higher high, which means it breaks the A price level, and goes higher, signals to us that the price action is showing strength and many people will join this move to capitalise on it. Price reaches X price level and then in a couple of seconds drops to the M level. Traders call it a "flush".

Since there is no protection from it, there are certain ways we can avoid it:

1) Price channels

These price channels helped me so much that I need to explain in the book as well. First, let's look at what these channels look like (*Image J2*).

Image J2

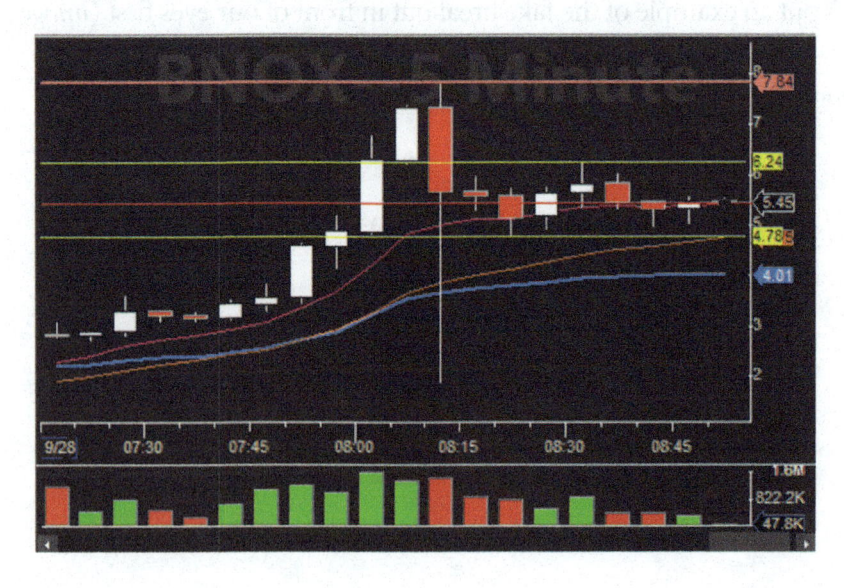

On the 5 minute chart (*Image J2*) you can see 2 yellow horizontal lines. I placed them manually and I adjusted them every time the price moved above the top yellow line or below the bottom yellow line. And because I am placing them as "global" lines, they are automatically put on my 1 minute chart (*Image J3*).

Image J3

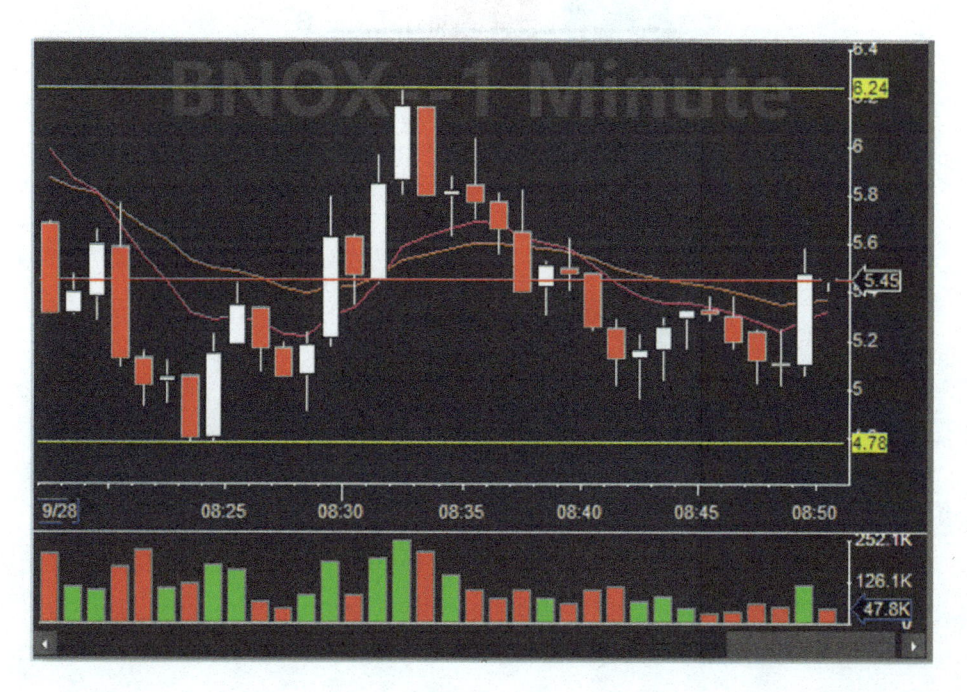

If you look at the 5 minute chart (*Image J2*), you can see that the price surged up to $7.84 and then went back down. Ignore the long bottom wick on the big red candle because it's just a bad print which happens with every stock at 8:00ish AM.

2) So when the price moved down and went into the consolidation (*Image J2*), I didn't expect the price to go up again soon because of how big the pullback was. As a general rule, the more price pulls back, the higher chance of a false breakout to happen.

Image J4

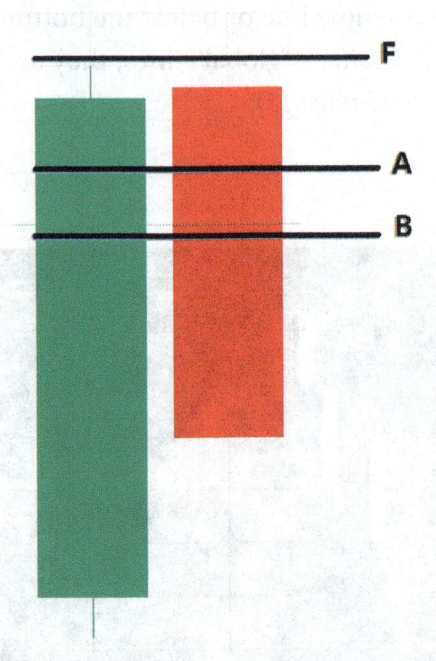

In the picture above (*Image J4*) you can see I have marked different price levels. This applies to both, 1 minute and 5 minute charts, especially when I am trading micro pullbacks on the surging stock on 1 minute chart, or looking for ACBD/Bull Flag on 5 minute chart.

F- The high of the previous candle;

If the price holds in the area between F and A, it's less likely that the price action will make a fake breakout. It still might happen and you need to be ready for it.

If the price falls down to the area between A and B, I will be more cautious. I would still look for a possibility to enter a trade, but Level 2 and the price action would need to send me strong signals.

DAY TRADING

And if the price falls down below the B price level, I start putting price action into the channels (yellow lines), and most of the time I will wait for the price to come back to the F price level.

Price level F is always the same, the high of the previous candle while A and B are more discretionary. If I would need to place numbers on it, I would say price level A is roughly 20% from the previous candle high, and price level B is around 35% from the previous candle high. It's really hard to give such numbers because it depends a lot on how the price actions are trading, volume and Level 2.

Coming back to the price channels. I draw horizontal lines on the pivot points of the pullback (*Image J5*).

Image J5

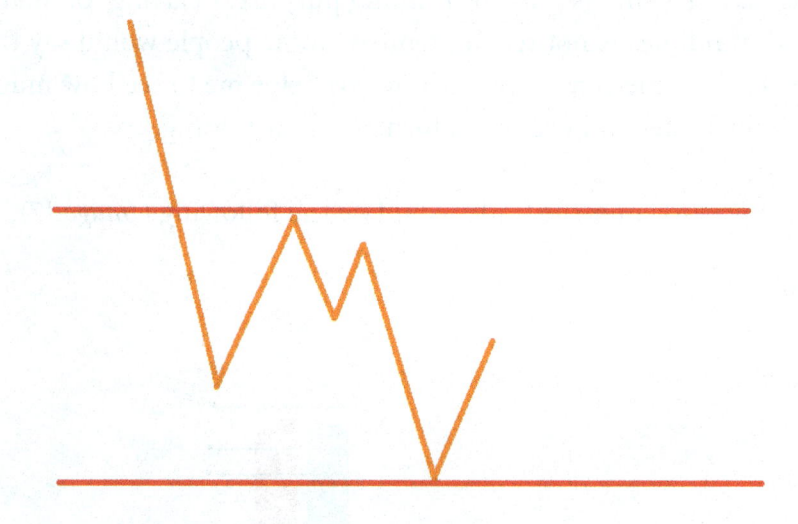

Most of the time I would never place a trade when the price would be breaking these pivot point levels. But let's assume the price made a fake breakout and because of that, I will adjust my channel lines (*Image J6*).

Image J6

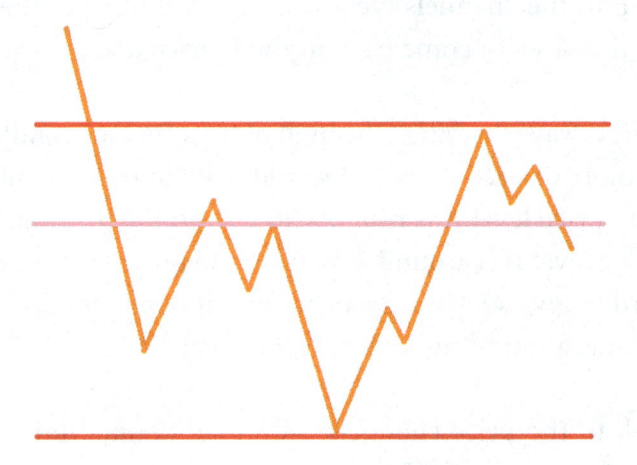

You can see the bottom channel line is still in the same place, but the top red one has moved higher. The pink shows where the previous red line was placed. (Pink is only for training purposes) Having too many lines and trendlines is not recommended. Some people would say the bottom channel line is not needed, but this helps me to see how much the price fluctuates and use this information for trading.

The safest way to enter the trade would be the following (*Image J7*).

Image J7

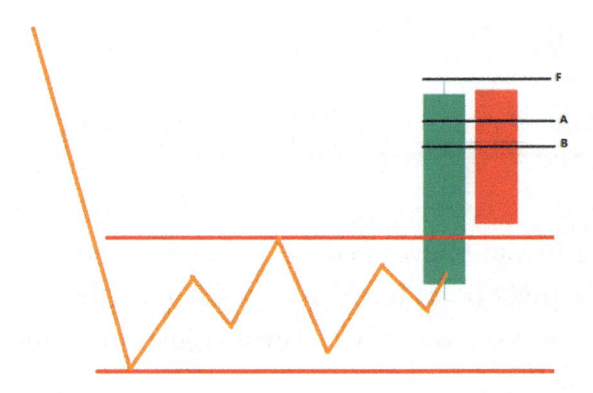

I would wait until the price breaks out of the channel, surges up, then pullbacks, and that would be the moment I would look and enter the trade based on entry signals that we learned before.

3) Checking previous candles that formed on that day

I would focus on the most recent price action, like 30 minutes or even less. Mostly it would be from the start of the price move. If I see that there are many examples of prices going up and then suddenly drops down and flushes, I will be more careful before placing my order. Of course, there will be times that no matter how careful you are, you will still get flushed.

Another important point to note, the candle doesn't have to be a big red one. A shooting star could be another great example of a flush.

Here is an example of me getting flushed. You will notice that I did have another position at the bottom of the flush, but I highly suggest not doing it if you are not experienced with it. And the reason I don't explain this strategy is because the risk is not worth the reward (*Image J8*).

Image J8

In the following example, you can see that the flush happened when the price was making a new High of the day, but then turned around and flushed down. The shooting star candle doesn't matter, red or green one, show us that this stock made a "flush" recently. If I saw this chart for the first time, I would be very very cautious before trading it (Image J9).

Image J9

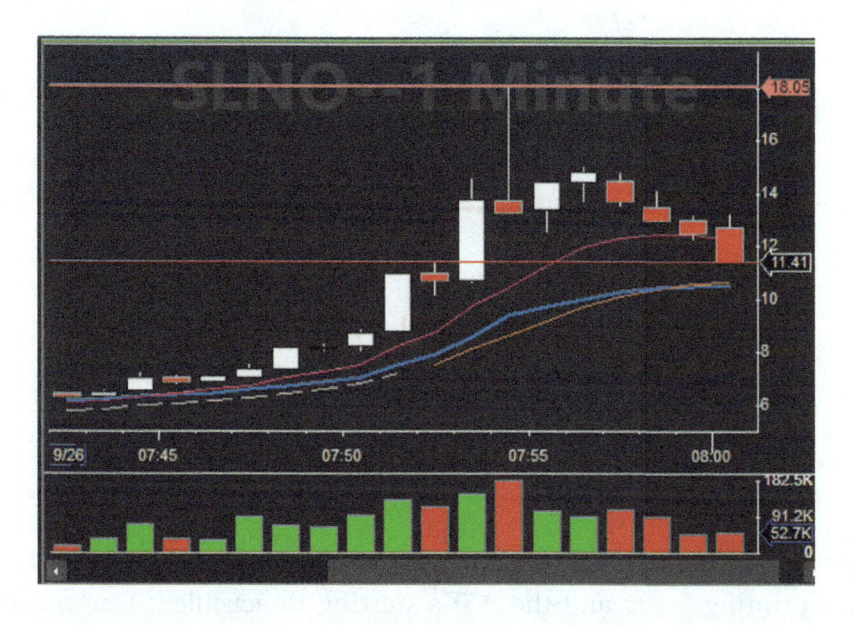

Furthermore, we can predict "flushes" by watching Level 2. Let's look at another homemade Level 2 where you can see a good looking Level 2 which has orders at every price level.

Image J10

BID	SIZE	ASK	SIZE
5.79	8	5.80	2
5.79	3	5.81	1
5.78	7	5.81	4
5.77	6	5.82	2
5.77	4	5.83	4
5.76	12	5.84	9
5.76	6	5.84	5

The price is currently at the top of the trading channel and about to break out (*Image J11*).

Image J11

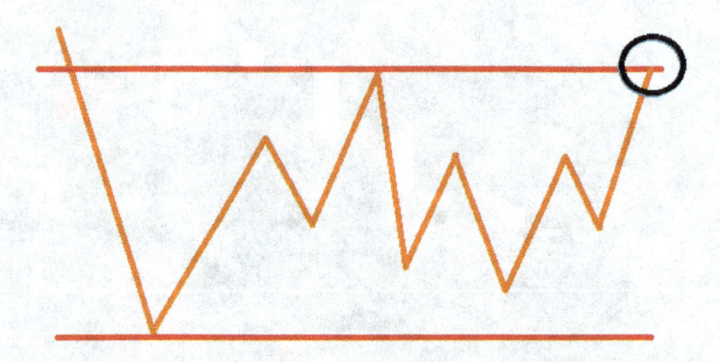

Since we are at the breakout point, we can notice that the Time & Sales start printing faster and the ASKs starting to get filled. Few seconds later we have a Level 2 looking like this (*Image J12*).

Image J12

BID	SIZE	ASK	SIZE
5.79	8	5.85	2
5.79	3	5.86	1
5.78	7	5.86	4
5.77	6	5.87	2
5.77	4	5.89	4
5.76	12	5.90	9
5.76	6	5.91	5

As we can see, the price on the ASK has moved up, but on the BID it stayed the same. This shows to us that the move up is not being

DAY TRADING

supported by the BIDs or the price is being marked higher by the market makers. In such a situation I would stay away from placing an order because most likely the price will surge down and will wipe some of the BIDs moving the price even lower than it was.

And lastly, this is the most common false breakout in the market (*Image J13*).

Image J13

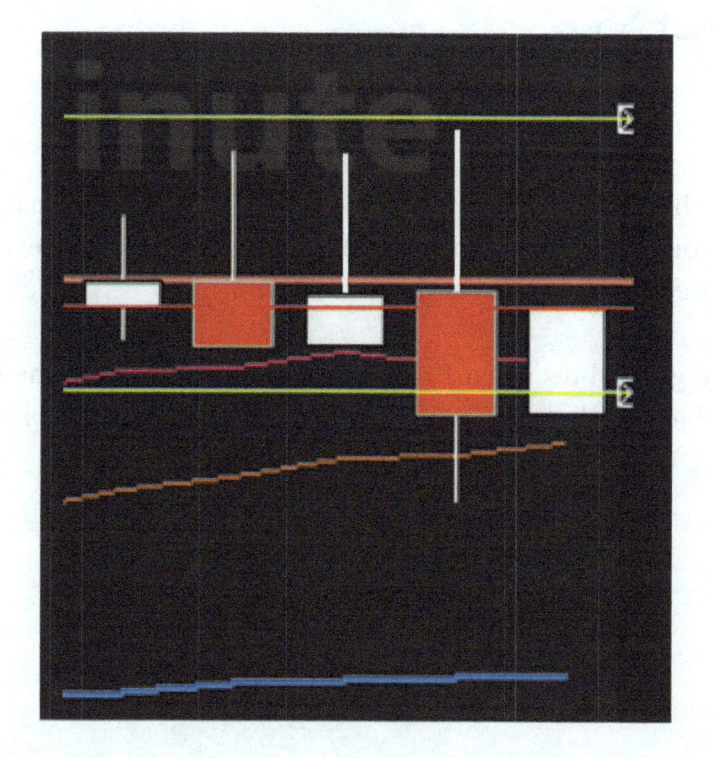

As you can see in the (*Image J13*), the pink line was the high of the pre-market. It was a very important level, but the way the price moved at that level was an absolute nightmare. Whenever you see at least two wicks to the upside, but the candles still close below a certain price level - move away from such a stock or at least wait until it stops trading in that price channel.

119

CHAPTER 12

EXAMPLE AND MY THOUGHT PROCESS

I hope this example will provide you with a lot of information and help you to set up your own strategy. It doesn't have to be everything step by step, use what works the best for you.

First thing I will do when I sit at my computer is check the scanner to see which stocks are most suitable for my trading style (*Image K1*).

DAY TRADING

Image K1

Symbol	Price ($)	Gap (%)	Flt (Shr)	Vol Today (Shr)	Vol 5 Min (%)	Earn Date (Dys)
BNOX	5.19	426.9		27.53M	22,158.8	
BXRX	0.6084	102.8	8,770,460	15.40M	88,063.2	
CHS	7.49	62.5	118.50M	7,075,862	10,085.2	-21.75
GRTS	1.50	26.1	84.50M	5,325,859	587.6	30.75
SLNO	24.29	17.5	8,094,720	199,709	94.1	34.25
CNXA	3.97	10.6	460,714	264,157	8.2	
OP	2.03	10.3	3,549,480	24,584	23.5	
BOLT	1.11	9.8	23.58M	1,123,565	2,269.1	30.75
SPI	0.9250	9.2	22.47M	10,798	0.0	
CXAI	1.68	8.4	7,601,660	149,944	29.3	29.75
GME	18.52	8.0	265.52M	525,327	44.8	-15.25
PTON	5.02	8.0	305.65M	1,039,478	109.4	25.25
GWAV	0.7500	7.7	11.30M	140,146	29.4	
GMDA	0.9997	7.6	101.97M	58,791	54.1	32.25
GNS	0.9250	7.6	16.26M	276,523	4.2	14.25
ORGO	2.85	7.5	78.06M	46,111	3.1	29.75
BBAI	1.56	6.1	48.42M	72,983	7.7	30.75
AKBA	1.22	6.1	166.99M	5,898	0.0	25.25
ASNS	1.25	5.9	2,293,000	422,867	129.0	30.50
MODG	14.27	5.9	142.03M	7,876	0.0	25.75
ACST	2.93	5.8	5,167,380	7,802	65.3	33.25
SSL	13.52	5.5		13,371	0.0	
BARK	1.22	5.2	105.20M	10,696	0.0	30.75

From the picture above, you can see that my day started at 8:42 AM and three stocks were almost within my parameters. BOLT had some volume, but the float was too high and not enough volume to consider trading it so I moved it to my second screen to keep an eye on it. BXRX had a nice float and huge volume, but because the price was at $0.60 I moved it to my second screen in case the price moves higher and I will be able to trade it later. Last one, BNOX, had the highest volume of all of them, a nice price of $5.19 which is within my trading range. However, float size was not provided in the scanner. So I went to marketwatch.com to check the market cap (*Image K2*).

Image K2.

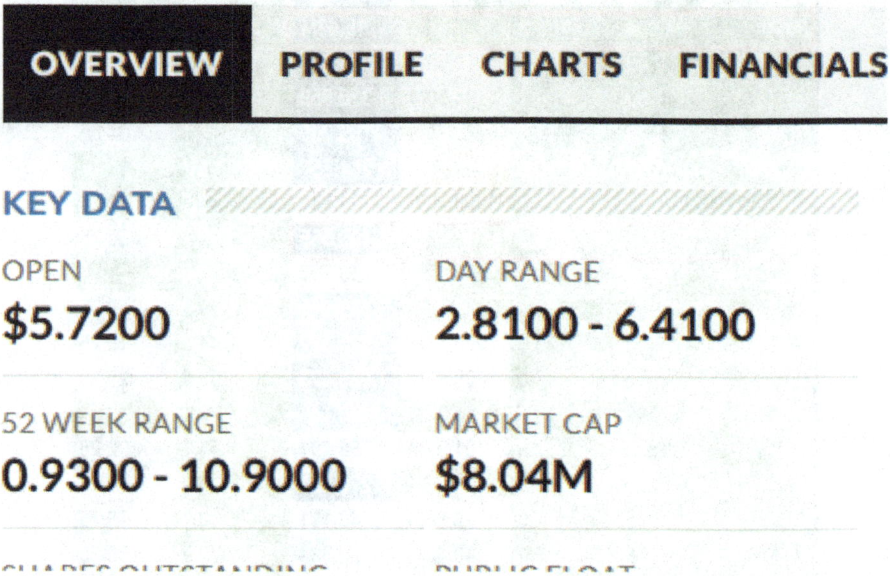

| OVERVIEW | PROFILE | CHARTS | FINANCIALS |

KEY DATA

OPEN
$5.7200

DAY RANGE
2.8100 - 6.4100

52 WEEK RANGE
0.9300 - 10.9000

MARKET CAP
$8.04M

As you can see the market cap is $8.04M which means the float will be even smaller than that which is perfect for me. We have a stock that is within our price range, float, gapped up 426% and have a massive volume. Let's pull up the charts (*Image K3*).

Image K3

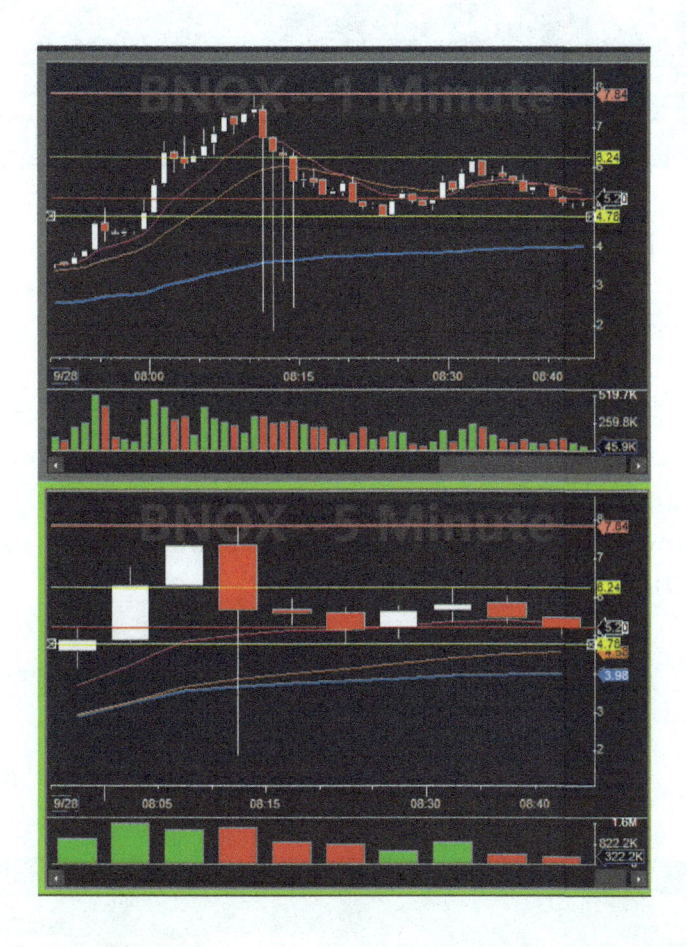

First, ignore the large wicks to the bottom between 8:10 AM and 8:15 AM because these are bad prints and happen to many stocks around 8:00 AM. Next thing I do is check the Daily chart if the price is trading between or above moving averages and are there any close resistance from the previous day's highs. Sadly, I didn't make screenshots of the daily chart, but for the training purposes we will assume that it is trading above all moving averages (and mostly it was because the gap up was +400%).

Next, I checked what's the Bid-Ask spread:

BNOX	↓	7.84 - 1.15		PCL	0.985
Last	5.08	4.095 (415.7%)		Vol	28,387,034
Lv1	5.04	5.1		Bid-Ask Spread: 0.06	

$0.06 is a little above my limit, I could look for an entry when the spread shrinks a little. It's not perfect, but so far the stock is fitting my parameters.

After this I will shift back to my 1 minute and 5 minute charts to look for price levels. I see that price went from $4.00 to $7.84 and now is consolidating on the pullback. Since the pullback is pretty significant, I drew yellow channel lines through the pivot points of that consolidation (*Image K3*).

For a few minutes nothing happened, the price action was doing its own thing, until I noticed this on Level 2 (*Image K5*).

Image K5

BID	SIZE	ASK	SIZE
5.04	3	5.10	34
5.04	2	5.15	10
5.02	5	5.15	6
5.02	0	5.15	1
5.01	1	5.25	0
5.00	1	5.32	1
5.00	1	5.32	1
4.89	1	5.34	1
4.87	0	5.39	0
4.86	0	5.40	1
4.83	6		
4.52	6		

Price levels on the BID are more concentrated at around $5.00 (provides good support) and the prices on the ASK are more scarce. If $5.10 would be filled on the ASK, we would get to $5.15 and then $5.25 pretty fast. I am very interested in this stock, but the downfall is that it is trading in the channel. Since it's premarket I will give it a go with a smaller position to warm up. All I needed was the price level for my entry. I looked back to my 5 minute chart. While I was looking at the chart the price moved higher, but I was still interested in it. What is more, the last two white candles (green candles) had pretty good volume which meant there were people interested in the price going up.

Image K6

The price was currently trading at $5.44 and the previous candle's high was $5.48. So the price level for my entry was $5.48 and I moved back to watching Level 2 and Time & Sales, especially when the price comes to that level. In addition to that, the previous two candles on the 5

DAY TRADING

minute chart had higher lows which is another indication of support on that price level.

After a couple minutes of watching Level 2 and when I saw the signals of entry I pressed my buy hotkey and got filled.

Image K7

DAY TRADING

It is really hard to explain why I entered in the middle of the channel, but Level 2 was showing me that the price should surge up in a moment. And it did, it went a little up and then turned around where I exited my trade on the way down.

Image K8

DAY TRADING

It was my own fault, I paid the price for the reminder that I should not trade when the price is moving between channel lines. However, I was still interested because Level 2 was still showing really strong signals.

The price went down, but it got bought up really fast which can be considered as a support signal. And again, the Level 2 was saying enter the trade now so I did.

Image K9

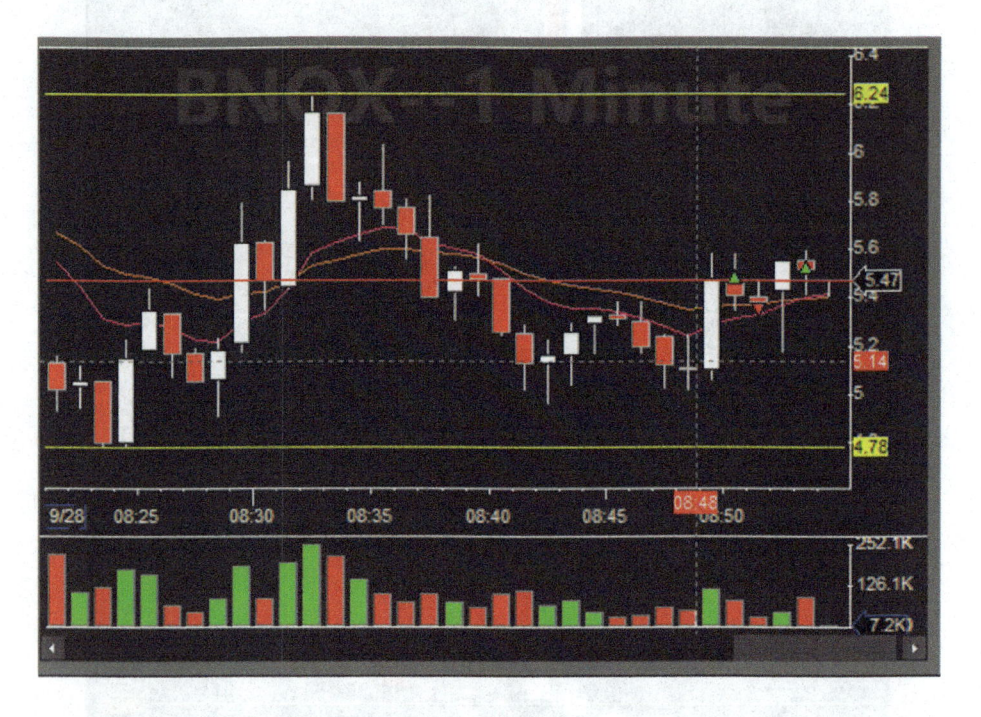

And this is how the Level 2 looked like (*Image K10*).

Image K10

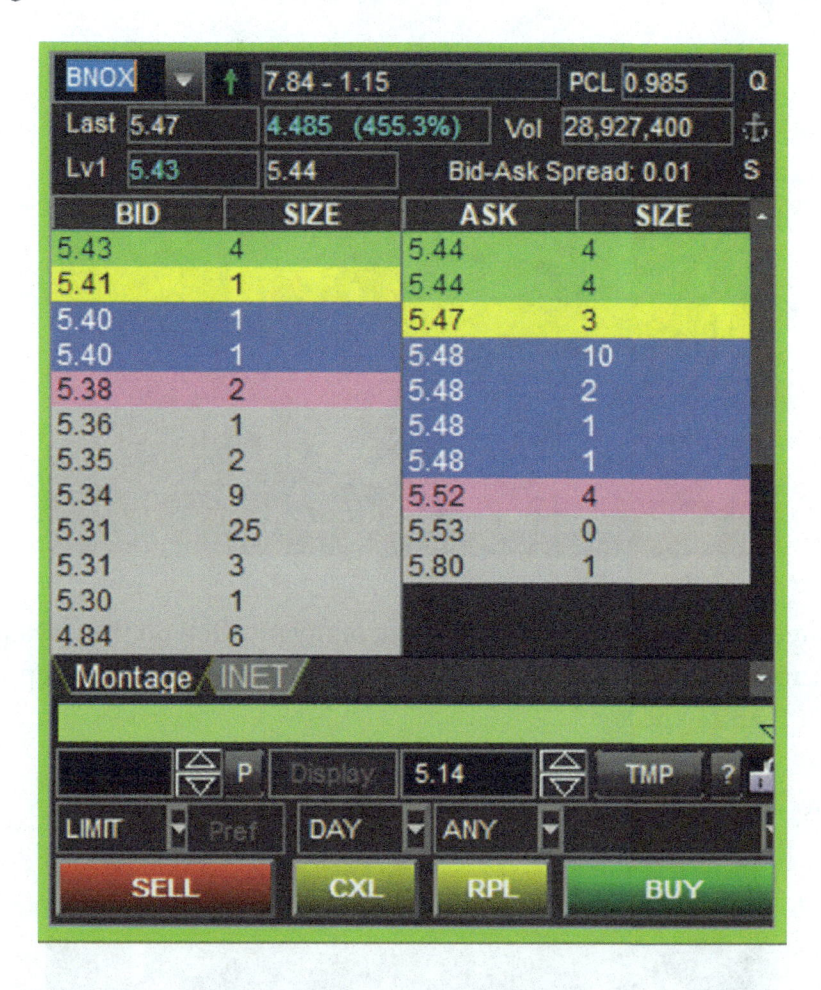

BID	SIZE	ASK	SIZE
5.43	4	5.44	4
5.41	1	5.44	4
5.40	1	5.47	3
5.40	1	5.48	10
5.38	2	5.48	2
5.36	1	5.48	1
5.35	2	5.48	1
5.34	9	5.52	4
5.31	25	5.53	0
5.31	3	5.80	1
5.30	1		
4.84	6		

Again, on the BID you can see orders at almost every price level, while ASK has less price levels, but larger sizes. But what was giving so much confidence was that after $5.53 the next price level would be at $5.80. At the same time, $5.40 was my stop area because the price on the chart and Level 2 showed that when the price comes to this level it holds it.

And after a few seconds, it did surge up and went up to $6.06, which is 60 cents move.

Image K11

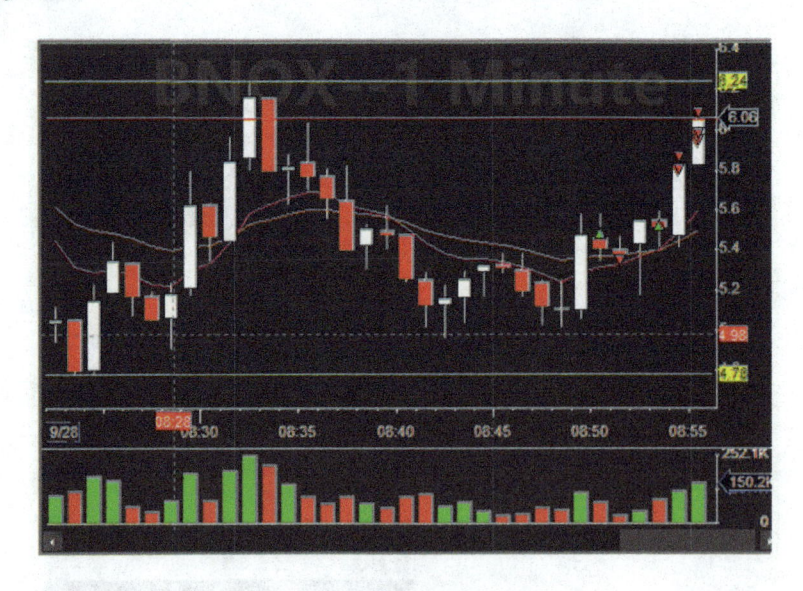

I exited my trades by lowering the size of my position on the way up to lock in the profits. But that's not the end of it. The price went up way more than I expected.

Image K12

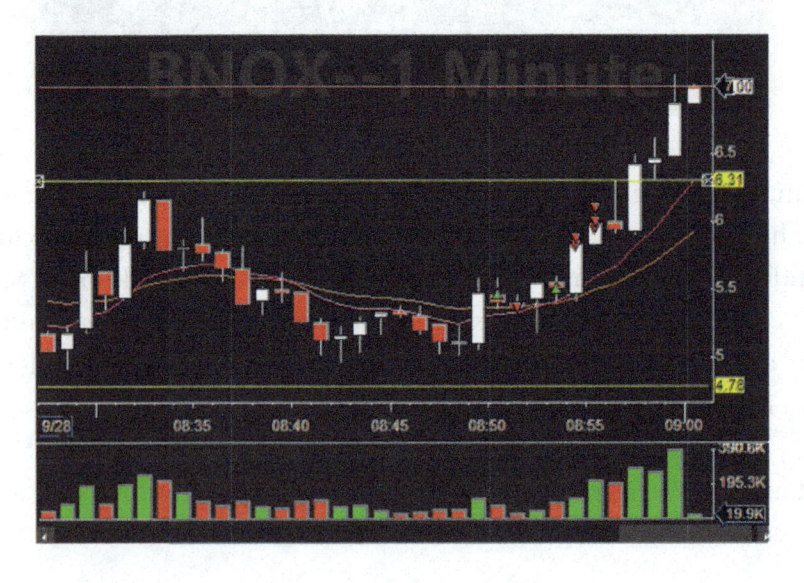

Some people would start thinking "If he held on longer, he would have made twice as much". Well, that's not my strategy and that's not what Level 2 was telling me. I would usually let 10% of my position to run, but because it was trading in the channel I took everything off. However, these are my trading decisions and I do not regret them. I made $0.60 per share on this move which is a lot considering the price of the share was $5.50.

So I closed my position, but I kept watching the price action and once I saw the price getting rejected, I started looking for different stocks to trade. 2 minutes later my scanners were signalling that BNOX is moving again and I missed it. It had over 30 million shares traded and it was just 9:00 AM.

Now I was looking for another trade, but first I needed a price level for my entry.

Image K13

Price moved back to 9 EMA on 1 minute chart and then got bought up back really fast. My entry level will be the high of the previous candle. And then I moved to Level 2 and Time & Sales. Once I saw the signals on Level 2, I entered my trade.

Image K14

I exited my position in portions on the way up to $7.10. But once I saw the wall (massive size ASK) on the ASK at $7.10, I closed my whole position right away.

As you can see the whole process that we just went through looks pretty simple, but the amount of the information you need to process and perceive is immense. And at the same time, that "information" is moving and changes when the price changes.

CHAPTER 13
EXAMPLES WITH COMMENTARY

Example 1

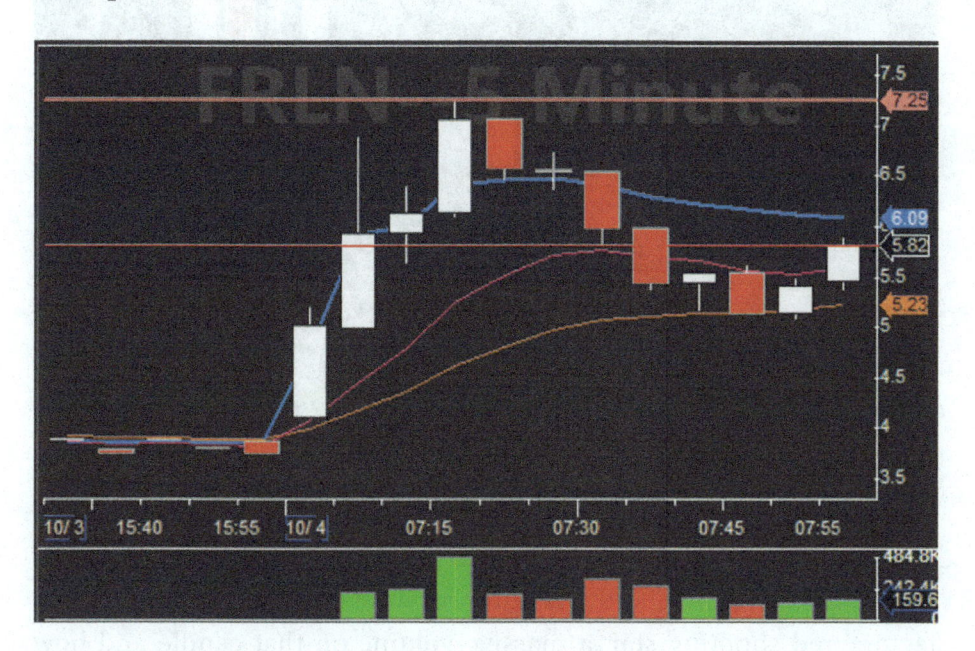

Example 1 looks like a perfect setup. The price surged up, pulled back and now the new 5 minute candle is making a higher high with increasing volume. However, I would be very cautious to enter a trade here because the pullback is around 50% of the initial move. In addition to that, the price is trading under VWAP which is another signal of weakness. The price might go up to $7.25 without me, but I have rules that I follow. Once the price gets above $7.25 then I would be interested in it. When I look at this chart, I think that there is a possibility for the price to go up, but there are more chances that it will trade in a channel for a while.

Example 2

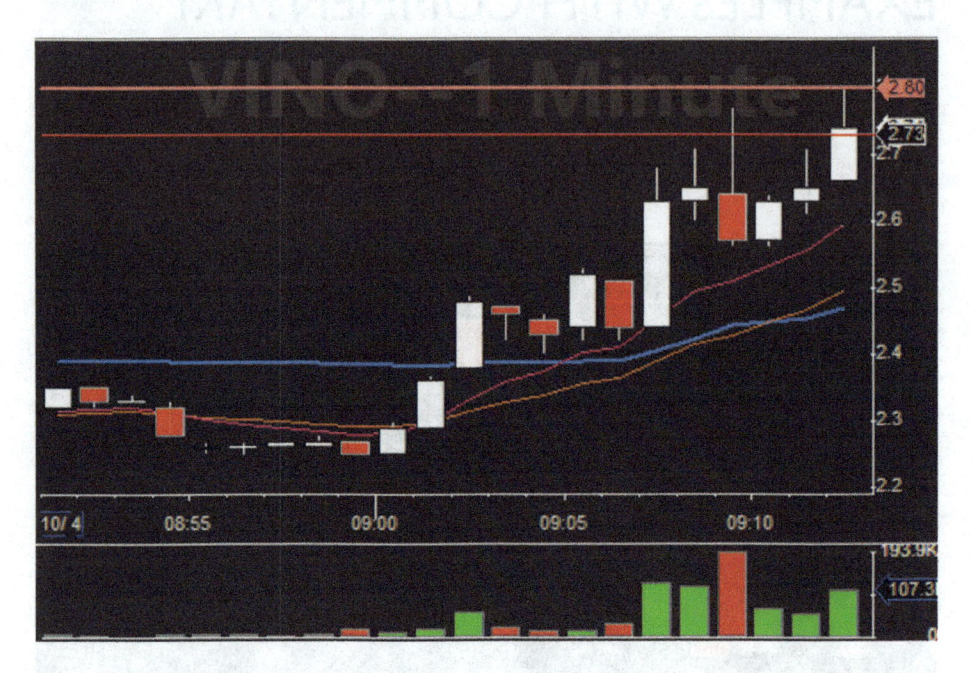

Here you can see that the price just made a new pre-market high. While it is tempting to look for an entry on a micro pullback, especially on the rising volume, still I would not place a trade. There are 3 key factors: red shooting star, a massive volume on that candle and how wicky the candles are to the top side. This kind of chart shouts at me that if I enter a trade, I will get flushed any second.

Example 3

BID	SIZE	ASK	SIZE
5.29	4	5.35	33
5.29	0	5.35	7
5.28	5	5.35	7
5.28	0	5.35	7
5.25	2	5.36	0
5.25	0	5.38	1
5.24	1	5.39	1
5.24	0	5.40	2
5.23	4	5.41	11
5.23	1	5.41	6
5.23	1	5.43	1
5.23	1	5.45	2
5.12	6	5.45	0
5.07	1	5.52	1

At the first glance it might look just as regular Level 2 with a larger spread. But if we look closer, we can see that the ASK side has more orders on every price level and the increments of price levels are $0.01 - $0.02. While the BID side has way less orders on every price level, the most scary area is when the price level changes from $5.23 to $5.12. This shows that the price can climb up slowly, but if it falls, it will fall fast and hard. I would stay away from trading this stock at this given moment and wait for the Level 2 to get more thick.

Example 4

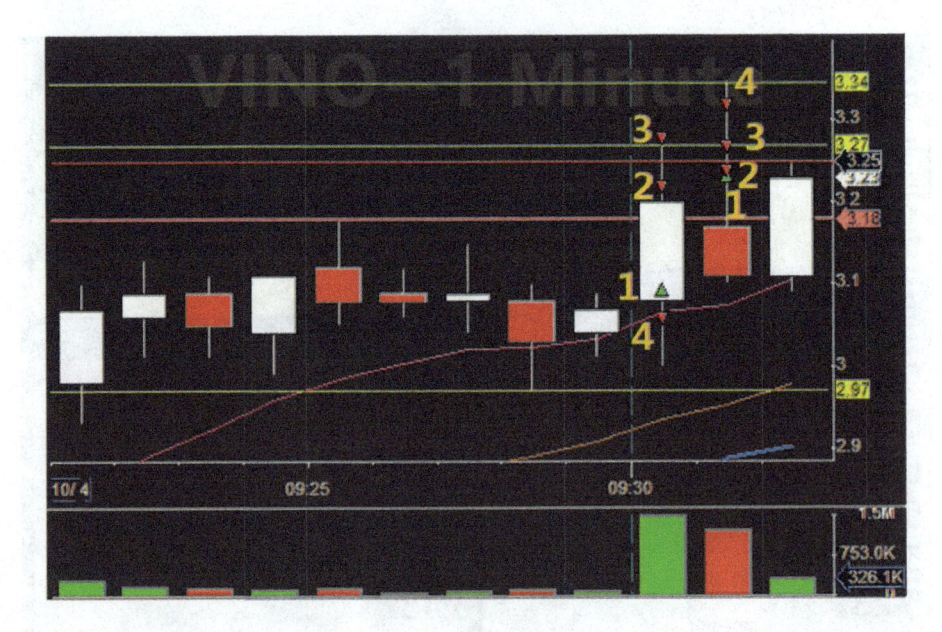

In this example I broke two of my own rules. This will happen to you as well, but you need to try to be disciplined and avoid breaking your own rules. I shouldn't have traded during the first minutes when the market opened and the price was trading in the channel when I entered the position.

I have placed two orders. The first one was based on the price action because when the market opened, the price went down and got bought back up really fast. I saw that the pink moving average was working as a support and the 1 minute candle was making a new higher high. I exited half of my position on the way up, but after that the price went down so fast that my breakeven stop had a lot of slippage and got filled at a lower price.

The second trade should not have happened at all, once I realised it, I reduced my position right away, and after that exited on the way up. When I look at my trades like this one, I feel disappointed in myself.

The trades were green at the end, but I looked at these trades as really bad ones. This time I didn't need to pay the price for the reminder, but there are times when I do.

Another important note to take, that during the first minutes when the market opens, Level 2 is going at the speed of light, which means it's really hard to see any signals, that's why I try to avoid trading at this time.

Example 5

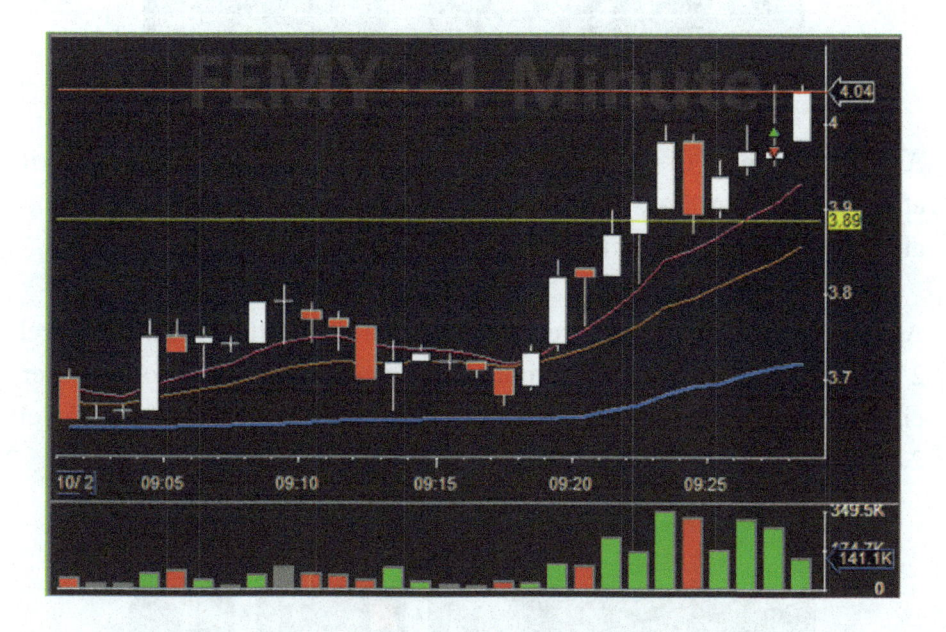

In this example I got faked out. After I entered a position, the price went up, but after a few seconds it dropped so fast that I couldn't exit even at the breakeven. False breakouts will happen and you always need to be ready for it. Especially when you can see that 3 candles ago there was a large flush down candle.

But it doesn't mean that this stock will be untradeable all day. When the market opened, I still managed to get a couple of nice trades from it.

Example 6

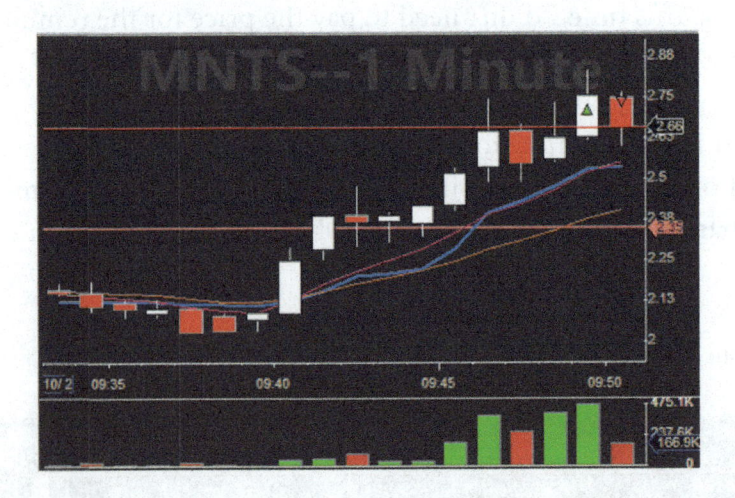

Another example of the false breakout, but this time I managed to exit at the breakeven. Yes, I still need to pay commissions for it, but you always need to be ready to react to the price level.

Again, the false breakouts are part of the trading. After this trade Level 2 was still showing strong signals and I was still looking for another entry. It took a couple of minutes, but once I got a go signal from Level 2, I made another trade.

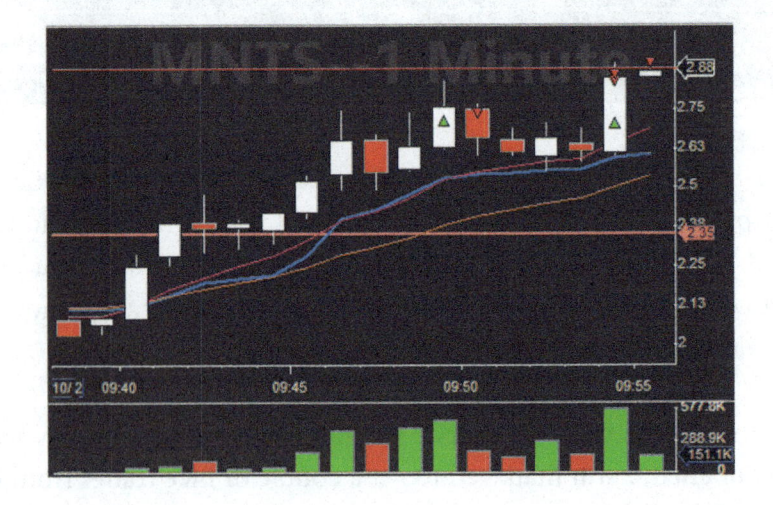

And a couple more after that.

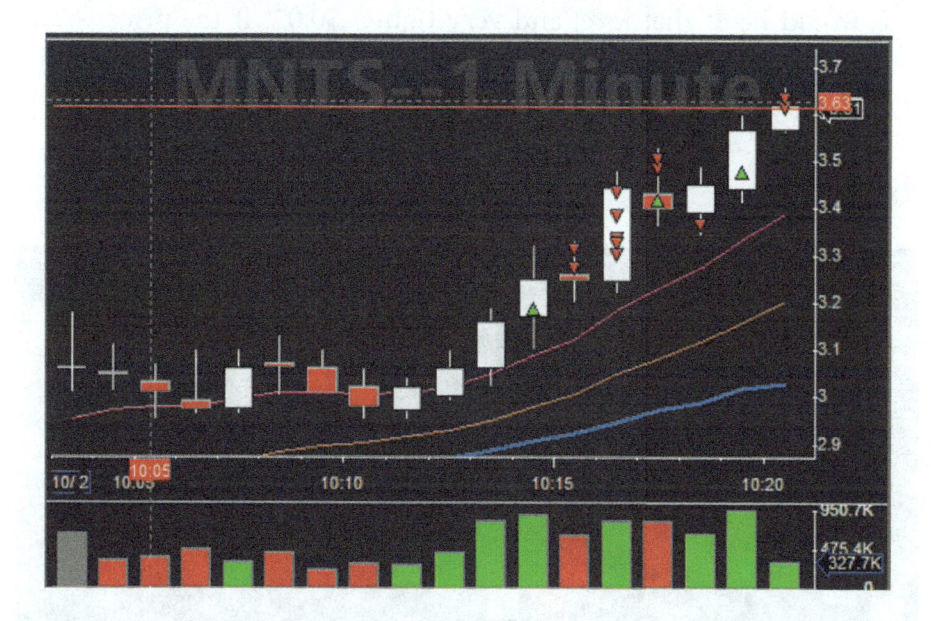

Example 7

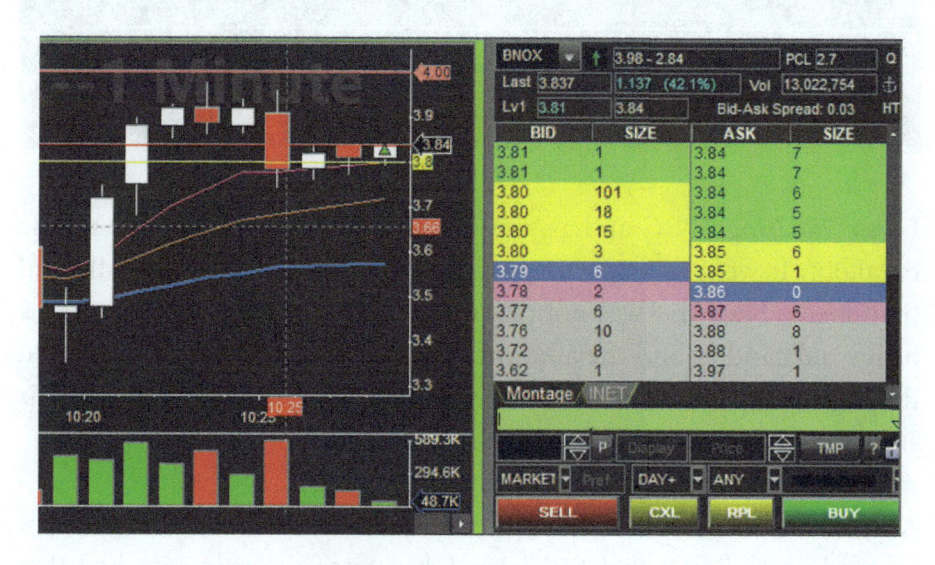

Here you can see that I just entered a trade where the candle is about to make a new higher high. But the focus is Level 2. You can see a huge wall on the BID at $3.80 which works as a great resistance. My stop loss would be at that level and very tight - $0.02. If the price would be going down and taking out these BIDs, I would exit just before the flush happens.

Example 8

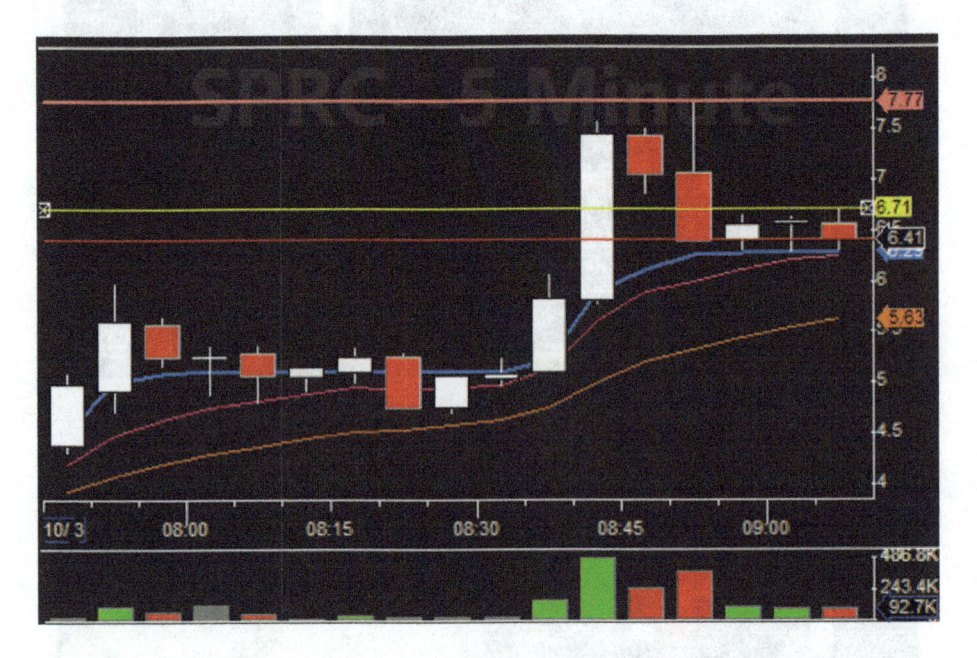

I was watching SPRC and as you can see the last candle made a false breakout. It went a couple cents higher than the previous candle and then flushed down. I was not planning to enter there just because of 2 heavy red candles and the amount of the pullback. However, I marked the high of that false breakout as a signal for myself not to touch this stock, at least until it breaks this price level.

And of course, later on the price came back with a strong move pretending to break that $6.71 level, but once the price reached that level, a flush happened.

DAY TRADING

I've managed to stay away from this stock, however, a couple minutes later I forgot about everything I knew and made a bad trade by not waiting for the first pullback after the breakout.

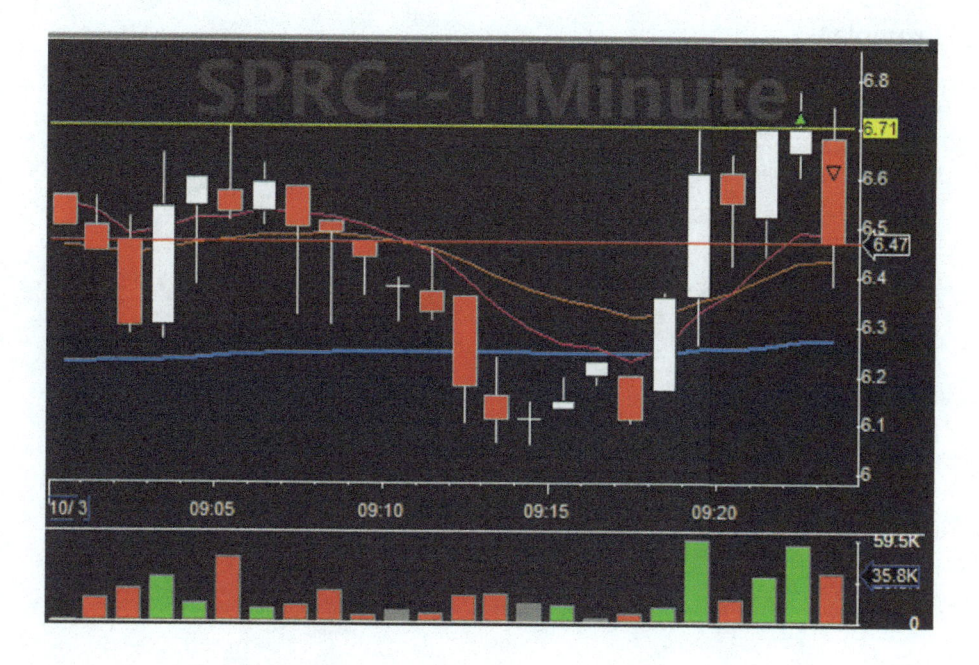

I paid my price for a reminder and didn't touch that stock again. However, for research purposes I kept an eye on it. Since it had so many prior flushes, I was waiting to see if another one would happen to confirm it. It took 5 minutes of waiting and another false breakout happened followed by a flush.

Example 9

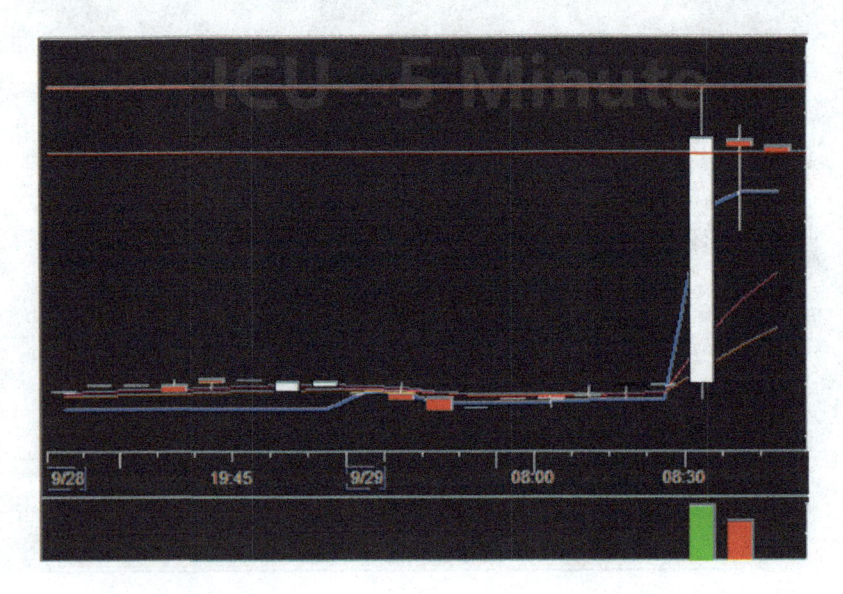

DAY TRADING

In this example I want to show how important "hammer" candles are. We can see a huge move displayed by a white (green) candle. The next candle went down under the VWAP, but got bought back up really fast which gives another signal of strong buyers. I wouldn't wait for the current candle to break the High of the day, I would enter at the break of the High of the previous candle ("hammer"). But this price level would be valid for another 2-3 minutes and if the price would be consolidating or going down, my entry target would change to the High of the day to avoid false breakouts. Of course, Level 2 would need to send signals to enter at that level.

Example 10

FEMY		2.21 - 1.88		PCL	1.52
Last	2.1287	0.609 (40%)		Vol	16,035,327
Lv1	2.12	2.14		Bid-Ask Spread:	0.02

BID	SIZE	ASK	SIZE
2.12	3	2.14	32
2.12	2	2.14	19
2.12	2	2.14	19
2.12	1	2.14	14
2.12	0	2.14	13
2.11	7	2.14	2
2.11	4	2.14	2
2.11	4	2.15	349
2.11	1	2.15	2
2.11	1	2.15	1
2.11	1	2.16	1
2.11	1	2.16	1

Montage / INET

We have another example of a huge ASK. My initial thought would be to wait until the 349 size at $2.15 decreases, and enter when a small amount of shares left just before the breakout. However, the $2.14 price level makes me a little uncomfortable. If we look on the BID side, the sizes of orders are pretty small, while on the ASK it's way bigger. This signals to me that this price area is really thick and needs a lot of buyers to push it through. Just by seeing such composition on the ASK, I would not enter a position just because it is too thick.

Example 11

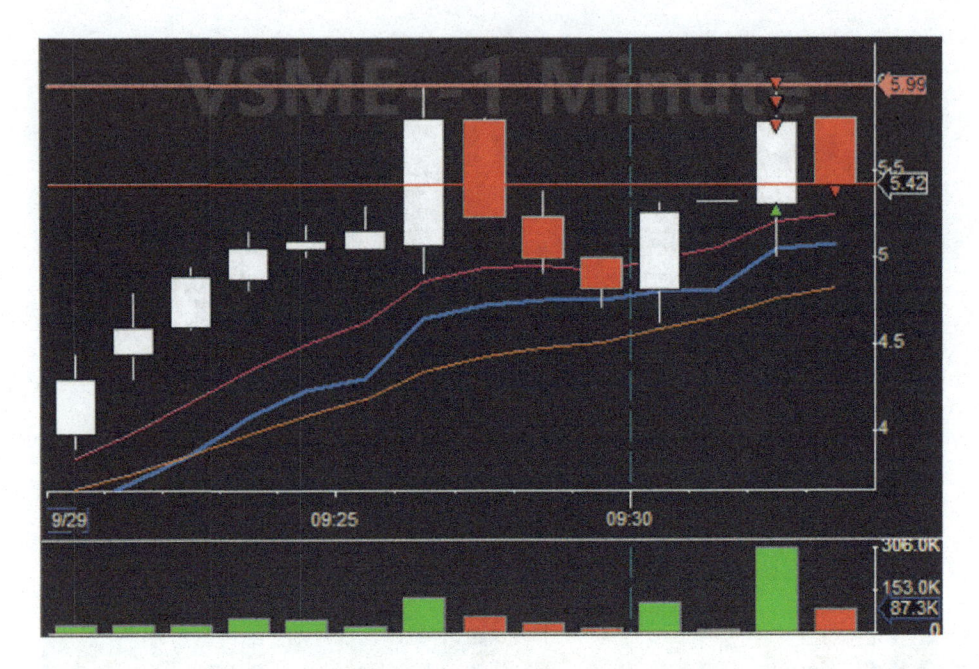

An example of trading after the halt. We can see that once the market opened, the stock went down, touched VWAP and got bought back up. I knew it's a riskier trade just because the price didn't open higher than the halt level, however Level 2 and Time & Sales were showing me strong buy signals. I closed most of my position on the way up and when the price started going down, I closed my position fully.

Example 12

Price	Qty
6.61	371
6.61	100
6.61	129
6.63	134
6.63	100
6.63	120
6.63	120
6.61	300
6.61	69
6.61	120
6.61	300
6.57	220
6.58	80

You can see that Time & Sales are showing green orders going through. I wanted to touch on this subject a little bit. Some traders watch Time & Sales and look for the price prints above the current ASK. Let's look at Level 2.

BID	SIZE	ASK	SIZE
6.59	10	6.61	12
6.58	11	6.63	8
6.57	9	6.64	16

You can see that our current ASK is at $6.61, but on the Time & Sales we can see orders going through at $6.63.

I've spent a lot of time looking for a correlation between prints on Time & Sales that are higher than the current ASK and the price going up, but I couldn't find any consistency in it. Again, some traders use it as a buying power signal, however after spending hundreds of hours I couldn't find any equilibrium to support these prints as a buying power. Many times I saw prints higher than the current ASK, but the price went down. It's up to you how you will use it.

Example 13

You can see I entered position early while the price was under moving averages and under VWAP. Ignore my trades because these are not momentum trades except the ones I entered above $0.65.

DAY TRADING

The main focus here is the price level - $0.70. As you can see the price came to that level many times, but couldn't push through. However, many traders lost money because they thought the price would definitely break that $0.70 level. Let's focus on the last candle. We can see it is at $0.70 level, the price action shows that price was moving on higher volume and ready to break that price level. Let's take a look at Level 2 and Time & Sales.

BID	SIZE	ASK	SIZE	Price	Qty
0.70	9	0.70	42	0.7	100
0.70	5	0.70	39	0.7	300
0.70	5	0.70	39	0.7	481
0.69	10	0.70	38	0.7	70
0.69	8	0.70	26	0.7	100
0.69	7	0.70	10	0.7	100
0.69	6	0.70	4	0.7	100
0.69	5	0.70	4	0.7	100
0.69	5	0.70	1	0.7	100
0.69	1	0.70	1	0.7	1500
0.69	1	0.70	0	0.7	1650
0.69	1	0.70	12	0.7	100

We can see orders wall at $0.70 on Level 2 and Time & Sales are moving really fast while printing $0.70. It looks like a perfect setup to us, however I would not enter now just because how many times before that price came to $0.70 level and never managed to break it. First and second attempts to break through a price level is a valid setup, but anything more than that - something fishy is going on and we should avoid placing trades for that moment. And here we can see that the price went down again without breaking the $0.70 level.

DAY TRADING

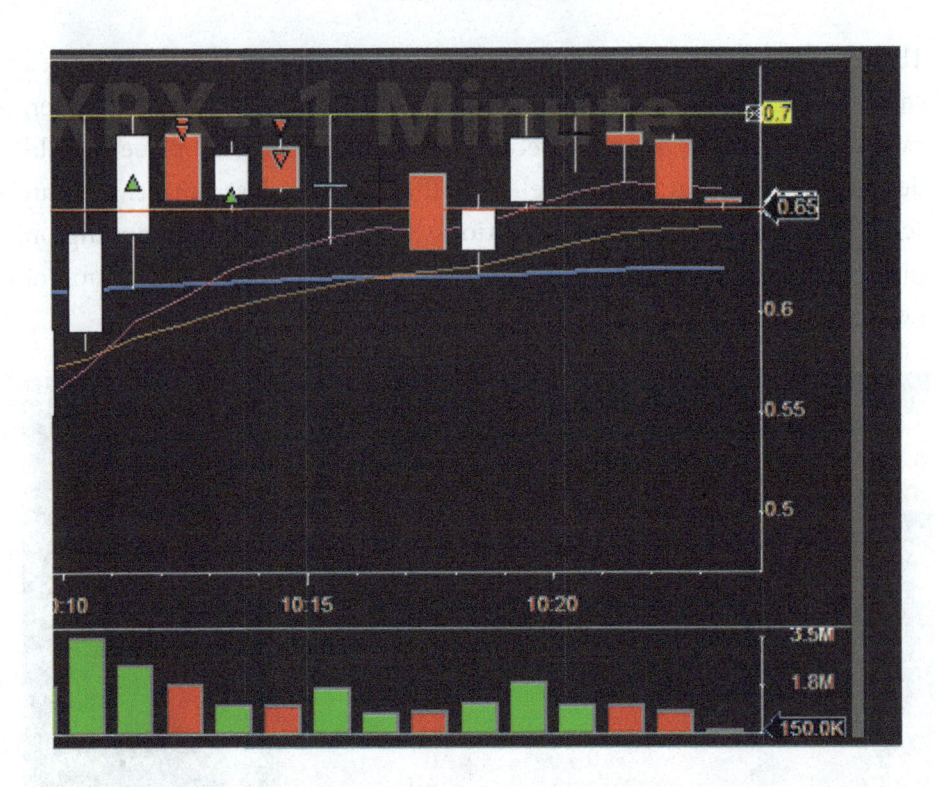

Example 14

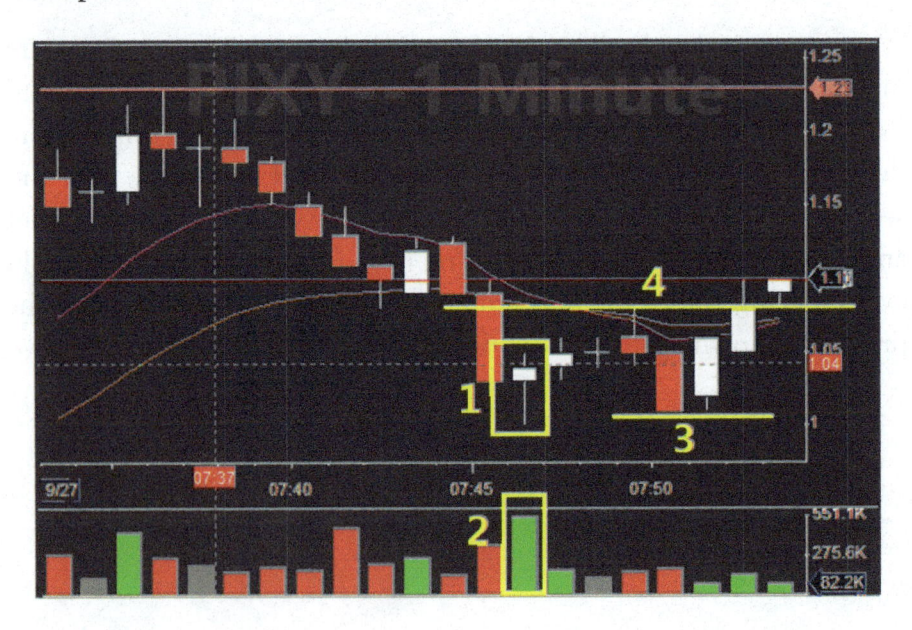

148

I want to explain more about what I see on the charts. We can see the price was pulling back and quite a lot. Because it pulled back so much, I will not place any orders, but I will keep monitoring the stock.

Then the 1 candle formed a hammer. The colour doesn't matter, but we see that price went down and then got bought back up which shows that there is support at this price level. The volume (2) shows that there was a big battle between buyers and sellers. Since the price got bought back up signals that the buyers won. I haven't entered yet because there are still early stages of the price reversal. We can see another pivot low marked as price area 3. Price area 3 is higher than the low of the hammer candle which shows us that price can't be pushed down that much and it's a signal of a strong support. When the price broke price area 4, I was fully focused on Level 2 looking for an entry, but I couldn't see any signals on Level 2.

Sometimes you will have a perfect setup on your chart, but if you do not see any signals on Level 2 to support that setup - don't place any trades.

AFTERWORD

I hope this book helped you to understand the market and the Level 2 better. As you can see the information that I provided doesn't offer a step by step guide because trading is not like that. It is a constant movement where you need to adapt if you want to survive.

I suggest you read this book at least a couple of times to understand what it is offering. You need to understand the concept of it and apply it to your trading. It took me a lot of time to gain this experience and I hope this will be a shortcut to your successful trading.

If you have any questions or suggestions, you can always email me at robertas.ceponas@gmail.com. I will try my best to answer as quickly as possible.

What is more, if you disagree with certain concepts that I provided, it is ok. Every trader is different and they perceive certain information in different ways. To some a buying signal on Level 2 might look like a selling signal. That's how the market works, there is always a seller and there is always a buyer. As I mentioned before, do not blindly follow what is written in the book, but spend time testing it and analysing if it works for you.

Godspeed to all.